TWAYNE'S WORLD AUTHORS SERIES
A Survey of the World's Literature

Sylvia E. Bowman, Indiana University

GENERAL EDITOR

SPAIN

Gerald Wade, Vanderbilt University
Janet W. Díaz, University of North Carolina at Chapel Hill

EDITORS

Eduardo Marquina

TWAS 396

EDUARDO MARQUINA

By MANUEL DE LA NUEZ

The City College of the City University of New York

TWAYNE PUBLISHERS

A DIVISION OF G. K. HALL & CO., BOSTON

Library of Congress Cataloging in Publication Data

De La Nuez, Manuel.
  Eduardo Marquina.

  (Twayne's world authors series; TWAS 396: Spain)
  Bibliography: p. 153–57.
  Includes index.
  1. Marquina, Eduardo, 1879–1946. I. Title.
PQ6623.A7Z63   862'.6'2   76–5796
ISBN 0–8057–6238–8

MANUFACTURED IN THE UNITED STATES OF AMERICA

TO ELENA

Contents

About the Author

Manuel de la Nuez was born in Madrid, Spain and came to the United States at an early age. After completing undergraduate studies at The City College of New York, he returned to Europe to study for a year at the University of Madrid and for another at the University of Geneva. He received the M.A. degree from Middlebury College and the Ph.D. from New York University. He has taught at Long Island University and Millersville State College (Pa.). Presently, he is an Assistant Professor of Spanish at The City College of The City University of New York where he teaches courses on his specialty, contemporary Spanish drama.

Professor de la Nuez maintains contact with the Spanish theatrical world through frequent trips to Spain. He is personally acquainted with many figures of the contemporary Spanish drama including actors, directors, and critics. He is active in the New York City Spanish language theater and has acted in many contemporary Spanish plays such as Jacinto Benavente's *Los intereses creados (The Bonds of Interest)* and Antonio Buero Vallejo's *El tragaluz (The Basement Window)*. Professor de la Nuez has also directed undergraduate and graduate student productions of Spanish plays.

Preface

During the first half of the twentieth century Eduardo Marquina was a favorite of Spain's theater audiences. Between 1902 and 1946 he staged more than fifty plays. Along with Jacinto Benavente, Carlos Arniches and the brothers Joaquín and Serafín Alvarez Quintero, Marquina was among a small number of dramatists who enjoyed a dominant position on the Spanish stage. Marquina also wrote poems, short stories, novels and an occasional article. However, the most significant aspect of the author's literary works is his drama; the renaissance of Spain's twentieth-century poetic theater stems directly from Marquina's efforts to revive the genre.

To date no book has appeared in any language that deals with Marquina's literary production. Critical studies on his works are limited to articles scattered in journals and to brief summaries in histories of Spanish literature and are mainly devoted to his theater. A few studies deal with the author's poetry, while his narratives have been ignored by the critics. Frequently judgements on Marquina's works rubber-stamp obvious second-hand information. There is a tendency among some critics to identify Marquina as essentially the author of historical verse dramas glorifying Spain's past. Such all-encompassing and imprecise views overlook excellent plays written by Marquina, such as his religious and rural dramas. Obviously there are many plays by Marquina which attest to the author's concession to the commercial element of Spanish theater. However, to arrive at a just evaluation of Marquina's drama and literary production in general, both positive and negative qualities must be considered, freed of clichés and superficial judgements.

Marquina is today a controversial figure in the history of Spanish theater. Judgements concerning this author are colored all too often by political and ideological considerations, particularly in Spain where the wounds of the Civil War of 1936–1939 are still a bitter and painful memory. Eulogized by the Right and censured by the Left, Marquina has been hurt by the lack of critical perspectives.

This study is concerned primarily with Marquina's theater. Because of the considerable number of plays involved, I have grouped them under specific classifications (e.g. historical, rural, religious, etc.). The organization employed, however, is essentially chronological, designed to trace the evolutions of Marquina's dramatic art. Each of Marquina's plays has been considered individually with emphasis given to those deemed more significant. His plays are placed within the larger framework of Spain's twentieth century theater. This study also traces the development of Marquina's poetry, especially the years up to 1910. After this, he devoted most of his energies to the theater and his poetry underwent few notable changes. Marquina wrote most of his short stories and novels during the early part of his career. In view of the fact that these works constitute, compared to his theater and poetry, a secondary aspect of his literary production, I have selected only the more significant ones for analysis. While Marquina's poetry and narratives are treated in separate chapters, his articles, many of which are still uncollected, represent a marginal aspect of his creative works, consequently I have chosen to omit them from the present study.

None of Marquina's works have been published in English. All translations from the original Spanish are my own.

I would like to express my appreciation to the editor Janet W. Díaz for her help with the manuscript.

MANUEL DE LA NUEZ
The City College of The City University of New York

Chronology

1879   Eduardo Marquina born January 21, in Barcelona.

1886– Primary and secondary education.

1896   Gives up studies soon after enrolling in the University of
       Barcelona. Works unenthusiastically for a commercial firm.

1897– Writes poems for Modernist magazine *Luz (Light)*.

1898   Does first Spanish translation of Verlaine's *L'Art poétique
       (Poetic Art)* for *Light*.

1898   In collaboration with Luis de Zulueta publishes the bullfight
       pamphlet *Lo que España necesita: menos guerra y más Guer-
       rita (What Spain needs: less war and more Guerrita)* and the
       dramatic poem *Jesús y el diablo (Jesus and the Devil)*.

1900   Publishes his first book of poems, *Odas (Odes)*. Literary am-
       bitions take him to Madrid. Returns to Barcelona after eight
       frustrating months.

1901   Supports himself through journalism. Second attempt to
       break into Madrid's literary world. Travels back and forth
       between capital and Barcelona. Publishes volume of poetry,
       Las vendimias (The Grape Harvests).

1902   February 27: Première of his first play, *El pastor (The
       Shepherd)*.

1903   Marries Mercedes Pichot in Barcelona, June 18. Son Luis
       born May 25, 1904. No other children.

1906   Première of *Benvenuto Cellini*, March 24. Has established
       his residence in Madrid.

1907   Publishes first short story *La caravana (The Caravan)*.

1908   First theatrical success, March 5 — *Las hijas del Cid (The
       Daughters of the Cid)*. Awarded the Piquer Drama Prize by
       the Spanish Royal Academy. He had now staged seven plays.

1909   Première, November 27 — *Doña María la brava (Doña
       María the Intrepid)*. Publishes his most ambitious and
       philosophical volume of poetry, *Vendimión*.

1910   Firmly established on Spanish stage, December 18, due to success of *En Flandes se ha puesto el sol (The Sun Has Set in Flanders)*. "World" première had been in Montevideo, July 27. Publishes book of poems, *Canciones del momento (Songs of the Moment)*.

1916   The historical play, *El Gran Capitán (The Great Captain)*, poorly received, March 30. Stops using verse and writing historical dramas. Accompanies Guerrero-Mendoza theatrical company on tour of Latin America for eleven months.

1918–   Writes a series of prose plays with contemporary settings.

1920   Returns to verse with *Ebora* in 1920.

1924   First performance of rural drama, *El pobrecito carpintero (The Poor Little Carpenter)*, March 29. He had now premièred thirty-three plays.

1927   Première, February 10, of rural drama *La ermita, la fuente y el río (The Hermitage, the Fountain, and the River)*.

1930   Initial staging of religious play, *El monje blanco (The White Monk)*, February 5. Travels through Austria, Czechoslovakia, and Poland. At Warsaw Conference of Dramatic and Musical Authors, elected president.

1931   Elected to Spanish Royal Academy.

1932   First performance of *Teresa de Jesús*, November 25. Elected President of Sociedad de Autores Españoles (Society of Spanish Authors).

1936   With wife accompanies Lola Membrives' theatrical company to Latin America. Outbreak of Spanish Civil War finds him in Argentina. Spends two of the war years in Buenos Aires.

1938   Returns to Spain. Establishes his residence in Seville which was in Nationalist zone. Prepares inaugural lecture for Spanish Royal Academy: *Lope en sus adentros (An Unknown Lope)*.

1939   Formally inducted into Spanish Royal Academy. Returns to Madrid.

1943   Première of *María la viuda (María the Widow)*, October 22.

1946   *El galeón y el milagro (the Galleon and the Miracle)* première, January 3. Last play by Marquina to reach stage in his lifetime. Receives the Gold Medal of the City of Barcelona. Heads Spanish delegation to presidential inauguration in Colombia. While in New York City on return trip to Spain, dies November 21, at the age of 67.

CHAPTER I

Life and Times

I Barcelona During the Restoration

EDUARDO Marquina was born in Barcelona on January 21, 1879 and spent his childhood and adolescence in that Mediterranean city, then undergoing unprecedented expansion.[1] The recent Bourbon Restoration in 1874 had brought political stability based on a system in which the two main opposing political parties took turns in running the country. Along with peace and stability came economic prosperity.[2] Cities like Barcelona, Madrid, Bilbao, and Valencia grew at a prodigious rate. Barcelona during Marquina's childhood was on its way to becoming Spain's industrial capital. The prosperity of the Restoration period was in a sense false, as its wealth did not filter down to the working classes who, having poured into the cities in search of employment, lived and worked under deplorable conditions.

The Restoration years in Barcelona witnessed the Renaissance (*Renaixença*) of Catalan culture. Its major figures were the poet Jacinto Verdaguer and the dramatist Angel Guimerá whose historical and rural verse plays possibly influenced the young Marquina. The resurgence of Catalan culture also reached the plastic arts and included the now world-famous architect Antonio Gaudí, and the writer and painter Santiago Rusiñol, who along with Ramón Casas helped initiate Impressionism in Catalan painting. Barcelona toward the end of the nineteenth century, due in part perhaps to its geographic location, was particularly susceptible to outside aesthetic influences. In Barcelona "Ibsen's plays and Wagner's operas were produced as in any other European city."[3] Its literary magazines played an important part in disseminating contemporary European aesthetic movements. An example is the magazine *L'Avenc* in whose editions of around 1892–1893 there appeared the names of Maeterlinck, Ibsen, Tolstoy, Barrès, Renan, and Nietzsche.[4]

In 1888, when Marquina was nine years old, Barcelona underwent a drastic change from large provincial capital to cosmopolitan
modern city. The catalyst was the Universal Exposition of 1888, the
first of its kind held in Spain. As the host city, Barcelona took on a
particular brilliance, with new streets laid out, others widened,
entire neighborhoods urbanized, public gardens created, and extremely tall buildings constructed. International conferences were
held, attracting important men of science, medicine, and business.
The Spanish Socialist Worker's Party also held a conference and
established their labor union, U.G.T. (General Union of Workers),
eventually to play an important role in Spanish politics. Referring to
the Exposition, a friend of Marquina, Pedro Corominas has stated:
"The Universal Exposition of 1888 made a deep impression on me. I
believe that most of the young people in Barcelona experienced the
same thing. It was a violent dose of cosmopolitanism. . . ."[5] Marquina, years later as an adult, looked back with melancholy to the
Barcelona he had known as a child and which changed so radically in
1888: "They took away the Barcelona of my childhood, and I haven't
been able to find her again. Barcelona was one place before and
another after the Exposition."[6]

The city's brilliance was soon to be tarnished during the last
decade of the century. The simmering social unrest among the
working classes burst forth in a wave of terrorism generally attributed to anarchists who during the 1890's had focused on Barcelona
as their principal area of operations. In 1893 a bomb wounded Martínez Campos, the Captain General of Catalonia. The same year
another bomb exploded in the Gran Liceo Theater, killing twenty
spectators and wounding many more. On June 6, 1896 during the
Corpus Christi procession, an explosive was thrown killing ten
people. After this last terrorist act, the police arrested many, who
were kept in the Montjuich fortress prison where they were tor-
tured. The "Montjuich" trial ended in 1897 with five condemned to
death.[7] The young Marquina was one of the many who protested
and asked for a review of the trial.[8]

During the last decade of the century, Spain was heading toward
the disastrous war of 1898 with the United States. In 1895 an insur-
rection had broken out in Cuba and was brutally suppressed. Two
years later the head of the government, Cánovas del Castillo, was
assassinated in the Catalan spa of Santa Agueda by an Italian anarchist, further aggravating the situation in Spain. The Spanish-

American War resulted in Spain's losing the last vestiges of her once vast overseas empire — Puerto Rico, Cuba, and the Philippines. Eduardo Marquina was nineteen years old at the time.

II *Early Years*

Eduardo Marquina was the second of seven children. His father, Luis Marquina, had come to Barcelona from his native Zaragoza in search of employment. Although his mother was born in Barcelona, her family was originally from León. Don Luis Marquina was employed in a commercial firm whose offices occupied the second floor of the building in which the family lived. In 1886 Eduardo entered the Christian School run by French religious brothers. Don Luis originally wanted his son to continue in his footsteps and be a businessman. However, after two years he decided that Eduardo should follow a course of study that would lead to a university degree. Eduardo then enrolled in a Jesuit school where he wrote as part of a homework assignment his first literary composition, a ballad dedicated to the Virgin Mary.

After finishing his secondary studies, Eduardo continued to attend literary meetings along with other young men who had studied with the Jesuits. Marquina has described the literary tastes of those who attended these sessions that were organized by various congregations: "We put together our literary passions, and it turned out that we were as one in our admiration for Zorrilla, Espronceda, Larra, Bécquer, and in general, for all the first line of our Romantics. We approached them by jumping over the Campoamors and Núñez de Arces who were closer to us in time, but who had paled and aged through use in our hands."[9]

His father's death, followed by that of his mother three years later, made Marquina think seriously about his future. Around 1896 he enrolled in the Faculty of Philosophy and Letters of the University of Barcelona. However, he did not complete the requirements for the first year. As Marquina tells us, he failed "General and Spanish Literature and "somewhat discontented he gave up his studies."[10] Marquina was able to obtain a position in the same firm that had employed his father. His salary of thirty pesetas a month was the first money he had ever earned. However, Eduardo was more interested in literature than in business.[11] In his office desk he kept books which he would read during his "breaks." Among the foreign authors of these books were Ibsen, Pascoli, D'Annunzio, and the Greek classics; Spanish authors were Saint Teresa, Unamuno, and the Catalan Maragall.[12]

III   *The Beginning of a Literary Career*

After two years as an office employee, Marquina left his position and, with his close friend Luis de Zulueta, started writing for the new magazine *Luz (Light)*. Marquina has described the magazine as "avant-garde" although he says that at the time it was called "Modernist."[13] In most of the issues, the young author published translations of foreign poets in addition to his own verses. It was for *Light* that Marquina wrote in 1898 the first Spanish translation of Paul Verlaine's *L'Art poétique (Poetic Art)*.[14] After some nine issues, *Light* closed down and Marquina and de Zulueta joined *Barcelona Cómica (Barcelona Humor)* which was, according to Marquina, a "routine and bourgeois" magazine that imitated *Madrid Cómico (Madrid Humor)*. During a few weeks, the two young writers dedicated themselves as Marquina tells us to "shocking the bourgeois" with their "Modernist lucubrations."[15] Soon, however, the many complaints by subscribers forced them to resign. Around this time Marquina and de Zulueta published a pamphlet entitled *Lo que España necesita: menos guerra y Más Guerrita (What Spain needs: less war and more Guerrita)*. This was Marquina's first publication.[16] Marquina's literary career was significantly advanced in 1899 when he succeeded in publishing a series of his poems entitled *Odas (Odes)* in *La Publicidad*, a Republican and Catalanist newspaper in Barcelona. Many of these poems reveal young Marquina's rebellious spirit. In *La Publicidad* and later in the Republican daily *España Nueva*, he published poems attacking the status quo in Spain. In 1900, through a fund-raising subscription initiated by readers and some stockholders of *La Publicidad*, Marquina published a selection of his *Odas (Odes)*. This publication provided him with a small amount of money which encouraged him to try his luck in Madrid's competitive literary world. In his memoirs Marquina has recalled this moment: "The century was ending. The so-called Generation of 98 was entering the world of letters. I, with my book that had a publication date of 1900, went to Madrid. My adolescence ended at that point."[17]

IV *From Barcelona to Madrid*

In this first trip to Madrid, Marquina met many of the day's literary luminaries: Valera, Jacinto Octavio Picón, Núñez de Arce, Galdós, Menéndez Pelayo, Echegaray, Valle-Inclán, Jacinto Grau, Maeztu, and Baroja.[18] The young author's literary credits were very limited and after eight frustrating months he decided to return home. Back in Barcelona he started working on some plays and continued writing poetry. From the beginning, Marquina had used Spanish for his literary works — the language of his parents. However, he did write *Emporium*, a lyric drama, in Catalan during this first trip back to Barcelona.[19] *Emporium*, which had music by Enric Morera, was never produced. Supporting himself by writing articles for various newspapers, Marquina, after finishing a few plays, attempted a second assault on Madrid. Finally in 1902 with the protection of the composer Ruperto Chapí, he staged his first play, a rural drama in verse entitled *El pastor (The Shepherd)*. The work's idealized, anarchistic ideology reflects the social unrest characteristic of Barcelona during the last decade of the nineteenth century. *The Shepherd* lasted only four days, after an adverse reaction by both audiences and critics. Undaunted, Marquina continued to write both plays and poetry. In June 1903 he married Mercedes Pichot, whom he had known since childhood. Luis, their only child, was born in May of the following year.

Between 1902 and 1908, Marquina searched for a type of play that could establish him on the Spanish stage. He wrote a few *zarzuelas* (musical comedies) with a rural setting and attempted to create a new type of Don Juan in *La monja Teodora (Teodora the Nun)*. The autobiography of the Italian Renaissance goldsmith and sculptor provided him the material for *Benvenuto Cellini* in 1906. Although Marquina managed to stage some of these plays, they were not very successful. Since the focus of his activities centered on Madrid, he decided to leave Barcelona and establish his permanent residence in the capital. For the daily *Heraldo de Madrid* he wrote a series of poems entitled *Canciones del momento (Songs of the Moment)* treat-

ing themes related to current events. It was around this time that
the newspaper *España Nueva* sent him to France and Italy as a
correspondent. In spite of his many activities, Marquina still experienced economic difficulties, since the productions of his plays did
not provide him much money.

Marquina finally obtained his first theatrical triumph in 1908
when the distinguished actress María Guerrero staged *Las hijas del
Cid (The Daughters of the Cid)*. Although the play's run was limited, the Spanish Royal Academy awarded Marquina the Piquer
Prize for dramatic excellence. The following year the author continued his pursuit of success with another historical verse drama,
Doña María la brava (Doña María the Intrepid). The play that
definitely established Eduardo Marquina was *En Flandes se ha
puesto el sol (The Sun Has Set in Flanders)*, first produced by María
Guerrero in Montevideo in July, 1910 and again in Madrid in December of the same year. Once more the dramatist was awarded the
Piquer Prize by the Spanish Royal Academy. The success of these
three historical verse dramas initiated the resurgence of the so-
called "poetic theater" in Spain. The three works also reflect a
permanent change in Marquina's ideology. Starting in 1908, the
rebellious spirit found in some of his early plays is replaced by a
conservative, traditionalist attitude. For the rest of his life, Marquina continued to publish an occasional volume of poetry, a novel,
or a short story. However, after the première of *The Sun Has Set in
Flanders*, he devoted himself mainly to the theater, and it is to this
genre that he owes his fame.

Between 1910 and 1916, Marquina concentrated essentially on
historical verse drama. In 1916 he realized that his theater was
becoming "affected" and decided to stop utilizing verse in his plays.
Marquina spent eleven months in Latin America with the María
Guerrero-Fernando de Mendoza company and when he returned to
Spain in May, 1917, he wrote a series of prose plays with contemporary settings. The year 1920 marked his return to historical verse
theater with *Ebora;* for the rest of his theatrical career, verse was,
with very few exceptions, his form of dramatic expression.

After World War I, in which Spain was not involved, Marquina
returned to Paris. His custom was to spend some time in the French
capital every year. Madrid was still his center of activity, although
he never lost contact with Catalonia. He frequently visited Barcelona and spent his summers in Cadaqués, a small coastal village

near the French border in the province of Gerona. During the 1920's Marquina wrote a series of successful rural dramas, two of which — *El pobrecito carpintero (The Poor Little Carpenter)* and *La ermita, la fuente y el río (The Hermitage, the Fountain, and the River* — are among his best works.

V Middle Years

When the author wrote his rural dramas, he was approaching his fiftieth year. In 1926 he was already a grandfather. Since the premiere of *The Daughters of the Cid* in 1908, he had built up a following among the Spanish theatergoing public and had become one of Spain's major contemporary dramatists.

During the 1920's, Spain was politically stable under the dictatorship of General Primo de Rivera. However, the problems underlying the social and political unrest that had characterized the end of the nineteenth century and the beginning of the twentieth had not been remedied, and they surfaced toward the end of the decade, causing Primo de Rivera to resign in 1930. The election results of 1931 convinced King Alfonso XIII of the advisability of abdicating to avoid bloodshed. The Second Republic was immediately proclaimed, and the lines began to be drawn for the civil war that broke out five years later. It is interesting to note, in relation to Marquina's traditionalist ideology, that in 1930 the Spanish Royal March was published with words by the dramatist. The same year, Marquina premiered his religious drama *El monje blanco (The White Monk)* and two years later, *Teresa de Jesús.* Both dramas, which are among his major works, might very likely have been the author's response to the strong antireligious feeling that was sweeping across Spain. In 1930, Marquina visited Austria, Czechoslovakia, and Poland. At the Warsaw Conference of Dramatic and Musical Authors attended by representatives from more than one hundred countries, Marquina was elected president for the next general meeting. As part of the tricentennial observance of Lope de Vega's death, Marquina adapted in 1935 the former's *La Dorotea (Dorothea)* for the stage. The following year, the dramatist accepted an invitation extended by Lola Membrives to visit Argentina, where that famous actress planned to present some of his plays. Accompanied by his wife, Marquina embarked for Latin America in April 1936. The outbreak of the Spanish Civil War three months later found him in

Argentina. However, his son and family were still in Madrid, which
was a Republican area. The name Marquina, identified as it was
with Spain's tradition and consequently to the political right of those
who controlled Madrid, forced Luis and his family to go into hiding.[20] Through arrangements made by Luis' father-in-law, they
were able to leave Spain with false passports. Marquina had gone
immediately to Europe, and in France the entire family was reunited. All returned to Buenos Aires where the author was able to
make a living thanks to his writings. While in the Argentine capital,
Marquina wrote new poems and made new collections. He also
began to write his memoirs in a series of articles published in the
magazine *Caras y Caretas (Faces and Masks)*.[21] Marquina kept in
close contact with the situation in Spain and actively supported the
Nationalist cause. In 1937 his activities included writing *La Santa
Hermandad (The Holy Brotherhood)*, a historical verse play which
reflected the situation in Spain and clearly favored the Nationalist
Movement.

VI *Post War Years*

In 1938 Marquina returned to Spain and established his residence
in Seville. In that Andalusian city he found time to prepare his
inaugural lecture on Lope de Vega for the Spanish Royal Academy,
to which he had been elected in 1931. The author finally presented
his lecture entitled *Lope en sus adentros (An Unknown Lope)* in
1939 and was formally inducted. During the 1930's and early 1940's,
Marquina's dramatic production decreased considerably, and those
plays he did write fell below the artistic level achieved in 1932 with
Teresa de Jesús. However, in 1943 Marquina achieved one of his
greatest triumphs when he premièred the last of his religious plays,
María la viuda (María the Widow).

On his birthday, January 21, 1946, his native city Barcelona
awarded him its Gold Medal. The same year he was again honored
when the government requested that he represent Spain at Alberto
Ospina's presidential inauguration in Colombia. Toward the end of
July the author started his last trip to Latin America. In Bogotá,
Marquina, who was already sixty-seven years old, felt the effects of
the high altitude and the many functions he attended as head of the
Spanish delegation. Marquina and his son, who accompanied him
on the trip, decided to return to Spain as soon as possible. However,

still on official business, he traveled to Costa Rica and Puerto Rico. Having completed his diplomatic mission, the author visited first Washington, D.C., where he read his poem *San Francisco de Asís* before the Academy of American Franciscan History, and then Harvard, where he gave a poetry recital. In November, Marquina was in New York ready to return home. However, the stress of the trip overcame him and he suffered a heart attack. The playwright did not lose his habitual optimism and spoke cheerfully to friends who visited him about future projects. Within a few days he had another attack, and this time his heart gave in. Eduardo Marquina died in New York City on November 21, 1946. His mortal remains were returned to Spain on the steamship *Marqués de Comillas.*

VII *"Generation of 98" and "Modernism"*

Marquina began his literary career around the start of the century. The main writers of the time have been grouped somewhat arbitrarily under the labels of "Generation of 98" and "Modernism."[22] Studies dealing with both concepts have reached voluminous proportions in the attempt to define them — the definitions vary greatly — and to label writers as belonging to one group or another. The application of these concepts causes numerous difficulties since frequently both currents are found in the same writer, as in Marquina's case.[23] Marquina himself apparently never formally acknowledged or denied belonging to either classification.

Jeschke describes Marquina as a "sympathizer" of the "Generation of 98."[24] Pedro Salinas, in an article in which he studies both "Generation of 98" and "Modernism," does not include Marquina in either of the lists of writers that he situates within these two currents. However, in the same article he does mention Marquina in a section devoted to the *"novecentista"* theater as the "best" creator of verse plays dealing with national themes.[25] In another study he states that Marquina's poetry places him in "the first rank of Modernism."[26] Pedro Laín Entralgo indicates that there exists "a generation of Spaniards subsequent to the so-called '98'." He places Marquina within this group along with José Ortega y Gasset, Eugenio d'Ors, Ramón Pérez de Ayala, Gregorio Marañón, Manuel Azaña, and Julio Rey Pastor.[27] Luis Granjel, however, sees Marquina among the "Modernists" along with such writers as Rubén Darío, Salvador Rueda, Benavente, Valle-Inclán, Villaespesa, Mar-

tínez Sierra, Juan Ramón Jiménez, Gabriel Miró, and Manuel
Machado.[28] Guillermo Díaz-Plaja distinguishes two groups within
each concept and includes Marquina in the "second group" of the
"Modernist generation" with Manuel Machado, Villaespesa, Juan
Ramón Jiménez, and Martínez Sierra.[29] Angel Valbuena Prat has
described Marquina's dramatic production as being part of the
"Modernist poetic theater"[30] and his poetry as having a "classic
tendency, within Modernism."[31]

A more valid and flexible approach to the literature of the times
and which we believe more appropriate to Marquina's work than
any attempt to classify him within either category is suggested by
Ricardo Gullón who has based his approach on Juan Ramón
Jiménez's theory of Modernism: "Juan Ramón Jiménez maintains
that Modernism is not a school, nor an artistic movement, but
rather, an epoch."[32] Following this lead, Gullón argues that in spite
of substantial differences, the element that joins end-of-the-century,
Spanish-language authors is a "common aversion to that which pre-
dominated in the immediate past."[33] Gullón rejects the "dissocia-
tive theory" between "Modernism" and "Generation of 98" defended by Guillermo Díaz-Plaja in his study *Modernismo frente a 98*
(Modernism vis-à-vis 98) and states that these two currents "respond
to different stimuli: Modernism is an epoch in Spanish and
Spanish-American letters, very complex and rich; 'ninety-eightism,'
a political and social reaction of writers, artists, and thinkers vis-à-
vis the Disaster of '98. It is wrong to place two heterogenous
phenomena in opposing positions, and we should accept, in any
case, the second as one of the elements of the first. Modernism gives
a tone to an epoch; it is not dogma, not a body of doctrine, nor a
school. Its limits are extensive and fluid, and within them fit very
varied personalities. (Modernism is above all, an attitude.)"[34]

Marquina's works must be viewed against the larger framework
outlined by Gullón. Only then can we reconcile the myriad facets of
the former's literary production from the anarchistic ideology found
in his play *El pastor (The Shepherd)* and in some of the poems
contained in *Odas (Odes)*, through the patriotic and "civil" poet of
Canciones del momento (Songs of the Moment) to the stylized, sen-
timental melancholy characteristic of some of his poems, novels, and
dramas such as *La ermita, la fuente y el río (The Hermitage, the
Fountain, and the River)*.

CHAPTER 2

Early Plays

I Introduction

IN 1902, the year Marquina staged his first play *El pastor (The Shepherd)*, Spanish dramaturgy was undergoing a marked transitional phase. Jacinto Benavente was already a playwright of note but had not produced as yet the major dramas that would soon lead him to displace José Echegaray as the dominant figure of the Spanish stage. Benito Pérez Galdós continued his struggle, initiated in 1892 with the première of his first play to reach the stage, *Realidad (Reality)*, to reform Spanish theater by breaking with the last vestiges of Romantic melodrama characteristic of the plays of Echegaray and his followers. Carlos Arniches had already established himself before the turn of the century as the foremost exponent of the one-act play, with or without music, known as the *género chico*. Also in a comic vein, but with their own characteristic style, the prolific brothers Joaquín and Serafín Alvarez Quintero had staged in the immediate preceding years a series of well-received plays.

The type of theater cultivated by Benavente and his followers on the one hand, and that of Arniches and the Alvarez Quinteros on the other, came to represent two of the major currents in the Spanish theater during the first third of the twentieth century. The third main current, which did not obtain the following of the other two, was the "poetic theater" whose initial impetus came from Marquina's first dramatic successes. These were not to come until 1908 when *Las hijas del Cid (The Daughters of the Cid)* first reached the stage. Although there is no outstanding work among these early plays, they are of manifest importance in understanding both the dramatist and the man. Critics have largely overlooked this initial period and have selected 1908 as a point of departure.[1]

During those early years Marquina showed a preference for plays with a rural setting, and it is with four works of this type that he began his playwriting career: *El pastor (The Shepherd)*, two "dramatic zarzuelas" — *Agua mansa (Still Water)* and *La vuelta del rebaño (The Return of the Flock)*, and *Rincón de montaña (A Place in the Mountains)*.[2] When the dramatist prepared the introduction to his complete works he stated: "I would have preferred that some of my first plays not be included in this collection. Namely, *The Shepherd* and one or two more."[3] The author does not give any specific reason as to why he would have liked to omit these plays and limits himself to setting forth reasons for including all his writings in the collection. However, it becomes clear from his additional comments that he is attempting to whitewash his early rebellious spirit which he has called his "original sin" (Marquina, *Complete Works*, I, x)[4].

II   El pastor (The Shepherd)

With the protection of the famous musician, Ruperto Chapí, Marquina was able to première his first play, *The Shepherd*, on February 27, 1902. The work contains a confused anarchistic ideology which reflects Marquina's youthful rebellious attitude. Dimas, the shepherd, whose name recalls the crucified good thief of the Bible, lives alone with his flock in the mountains. After killing a wolf that has devoured a youth, Dimas meets Magdalena, the daughter of Tomás, a rich man, and it is love at first sight for both. Magdalena's father accuses Dimas of the youth's murder and under threat of violence forces Andrés, his daughter's weak-willed fiancé, to help in his capture. On the night that Dimas tries to escape with Magdalena, Andrés decides to help the couple. The play ends with the arrival of Tomás who finds out what has happened and grasps Andrés' throat in an attempt to kill him.

The play, as the plot summary implies, is the work of both a novice in the theater and of an individual who has not come to terms with the world around him. *The Shepherd* is a badly fused mixture of different sources and influences, among others the Bible, Romantic literature, politics of the day, and Symbolist theater. The characters are badly drawn and are made to fit the dramatist's uncertain ideology. Dimas appears initially as a sort of unfettered Romantic hero without roots or personal history. Soon, however, he becomes a prisoner of love and a fervent propagandist of an obscure, idealized anarchism that longs for a utopian state of humanity. The shepherd extols the virtues of his existence close to nature without man-made laws or other obstacles to impede the freedom of his being. The twenty-three-year-old author proposes a world in which work shall be a labor of love and there will be an exchange "among all/of the fruits of a productive life" (*Works*, I, 37). However, for the weak to become strong, violence is necessary as in Andrés' case, and people will say he "died because ideas need blood/in order to expand and germinate" (*Works*, I, 58). Along with his concern for the play's "ideology," Marquina finds time to idealize the female figure. Magdalena is an embryonic model of many of the author's future heroines — all good, virtuous, self-sacrificing women with maternalistic feelings toward the men they love.

The play was poorly received by both audiences and critics and lasted only four days. In *The Shepherd*, Marquina the poet makes very few concessions to Marquina the playwright. It "is a lyric poem written in free verse and divided into scenes, that is to say, it is a work that can be staged, but is in no way theatrical."[5] During a good part of the drama the main characters give what amounts to a series of expositions dealing with justice, humanity, and other similar subjects without rising above the simplest commonplaces. Yet *The Shepherd* is one of the dramatist's more interesting plays if only for the reason that it reveals a Marquina that is largely unknown and that bears scant resemblance to the author of *En Flandes se ha puesto el sol (The Sun Has Set in Flanders)*. It also provides insight into an aspect of literary history that until recently has been ignored.[6] Marquina's name must be added to the list of those turn-of-the-century writers such as Miguel de Unamuno, Pío Baroja, Ramiro de Maeztu, and Azorín who adopted during their youth, each in his own way, what might be termed "radical" attitudes which they later abandoned.

III   *Other Early Rural Plays*

Marquina's other early plays with a rural setting generally follow convention yet contain some features that are important in the development of the author's later plays. In the one-act dramatic zarzuela, *Agua mansa (Still Water)*, written, as is *La vuelta del rebaño (The Return of the Flock)*, in prose with the exception of the songs,

Marquina utilizes for the first time one of his favorite themes: the
victory of "good" love over "bad." In *Still Water* the love of Rosa,
who is goodness incarnate, will triumph over that of her "bad" sister
Juana. This theme is inverted in *The Return of the Flock* where
Marquina places two brothers, Climentón and Gervasio, in a Cain
and Abel competition for the love of the same woman, Laya.
Climentón, who is the "good" brother, wins the girl. Marquina
obtained a minor success with *Still Water*, but *The Return of the
Flock* was a failure, due in part, perhaps, to the lack of originality of
the second play (essentially a modified copy of the first).

The last rural drama that the author wrote in these early years was
Rincón de montaña (A Place in the Mountains). Again, "good" love
triumphs but with a variation: two women, la Chorca and Rebeca
reach true love in spite of the village cad, Bruno. *A Place in the
Mountains* never reached the stage, and although the theme is
familiar, its treatment shows more of the practiced hand of a
dramatist than the three previous rural dramas that were produced.
The play is longer and more complex, and it is evident from the
stage directions that Marquina was beginning to feel his way in the
theater. There is a greater use of plastic elements to help create a
dramatic "climate." The author also makes use of a folk song as a
symbolic summary of the action, which is a device used successfully
by Lope de Vega and,·among others, by Jacinto Benavente and
García Lorca.

IV   El delfín (The Dauphin)

In 1904 Marquina interrupted his series of rural plays to write the
"historical zarzuela" *El delfín (The Dauphin)* in collaboration with
José Salmerón and the composers Juan Gay and Tomás Barrera. The
play draws on one of the legends that sprang up after the "disap-
pearance" of Charles, the son of Marie Antoinette. The Dauphin,
"Luis," unaware of his true identity, has been raised by Barón Claquín in New York City so that he might benefit from contact with a
free country. Word arrives of the Bourbon restoration, but it is said
that Louis XVIII is tyrannical. Claquín decides that it is time for the
Dauphin to know the truth and claim his rights. Once in France,
Luis succeeds in proving his identity and the King agrees to give up
the throne. However, when the Dauphin begins to exalt the rights

of the people, Louis XVIII has the "impostor" thrown out of the palace. The Dauphin then decides to join the common woman he loves at the barricades.

The Dauphin is essentially an ode to the rights of the people. In their eagerness to exalt these rights, the authors neglect the work's dramatic construction, so that, at times, the play seems more a political manifesto than a zarzuela libretto. The focus of the play is summed up in a dialogue betwen Louis XVIII and the Dauphin. The monarch exclaims: "The duty of a king is to defend his throne," to which the Dauphin responds: "The duty of a king is to please his people. . . . I want the poor and oppressed to be able to follow me into the Tuilleries and the will of the people to be my scepter" (*Works*,I,306–7).

In the case of joint authorship it is difficult to single out individual contributions. However, regardless of which of the two is responsible for the play's theme, the fact remains that Marquina agreed to collaborate with Salmerón on a work of this nature. *The Dauphin* (whose staging in 1907 was not successful) must be considered another projection of Marquina's youthful nonconformist attitude.

V La monja Teodora (Teodora the Nun)

In 1905 Marquina wrote in verse the "dramatic legend," *Teodora the Nun*. With the exception of *The Shepherd* and the songs in the zarzuelas, the author's plays had all been written in prose. *Teodora the Nun* is extremely complicated, confusing, and, at times, contradictory. In later years Marquina admitted that he was ill prepared to handle a play of this type and acknowledged the work's weaknesses, describing it as "a theatrical rough draft, a bit shapeless" (*Works*,I,1234).

In spite of the title, the protagonist is don Diego, a donjuanesque type who has decided to get married, although his adventures indicate no inclination to settle down.[7] His many escapades require a great deal of money, and he is forced to seek help from his bastard brother who is an alchemist. Nicodemo, who resents his half-brother, needs a nun's crucifix for his experiments, and don Diego attempts to steal it from Teodora and seduce her at the same time. From then on, the plot becomes hopelessly involved and difficult to follow. Teodora — who apparently has left the convent — has vowed to follow don Diego forever. At don Diego's and Malvina's wedding, the former kills his fiancée's father, don Pedro, when he objects to the groom laying claim to both Malvina and Teodora. Forced to escape, don Diego eventually returns to search for Malvina and is killed by Nicodemo.

Although the play was never produced, both it and the accompanying notes are important to a comprehension of Marquina's theater. In the notes, which are rather extensive and can only partially be reproduced here, the dramatist makes an effort to explain the play. Apparently, when he began writing the play, Marquina intended to condemn "legendary Spain," symbolized by don Diego. Nicodemo, whom Marquina recognizes as being contradictory in his makeup, was to be representative of the "disinherited classes . . . the reaction against legendary Spain; the constant and arid propaganda of a life of reality and of earthy Positivism: almost of 'Europeanization' . . ." (Works, I, 1236). In contrast to Malvina, Teodora was "above all, the Spanish chimera with cross and nun's bonnet as is proper in a good doctrine of regeneration. . . . She is Spain's traditional and reprobate past . . . another half of Spain's Black Legend . . . at the same time sacrilegious and devout, sensual and mystical" (Works, I, 1236). Malvina symbolized "reality; the true life without haughtiness or tradition rooted in legend; close to the earth from which she extracts a wholesome warmth of 'regeneration' and of 'truth' " (Works, I, 1236). The result of don Diego and Malvina's wedding was to be the union of this "regenerative spirit" with a Spain stripped of legend.

Notwithstanding his original intentions, as Marquina wrote *Teodora the Nun*, Malvina started to slip out of the author's grasp as she came into contact with don Diego and was influenced by him. Malvina, instead of eliminating don Diego's legend, exalts it. However, Marquina also feels don Diego's attraction, and this causes him to sidetrack Nicodemo and Teodora with their symbolic content and both he and Malvina "without noticing it, with the same love, fall defeated, with the same veneration at the hidalgo's feet" (Works, I, 1237).

To sum up Marquina's notes, we observe that the author's original plan was to condemn legendary Spain by means of a series of symbolic characters. In the legend's place he proposed a "regenerated" Spain that remained close to reality and truth. However, when some of his characters claimed their independence, his original plan became altered. Marquina waxed enthusiastic about don Diego's traditional Hispanic traits and the author ended up admiring the same legend he proposed to condemn.

It is interesting to note Marquina's efforts to place *Teodora the Nun* in an ideological area (i.e., "Europeanization" and "regeneration") kindred to writers of the "Generation of 1898." The fact that Marquina finally identifies with don Diego's symbolic content is a process common to other contemporary authors, who from a negative attitude toward the Hispanic tradition go on to defend it. With all the differences that exist between Miguel de Unamuno and Ramiro de Maeztu, and in addition to the gulf that separates them from Marquina, both these authors similarly abandoned their initial stance favoring "Europeanization" to exalt the Hispanic tradition.

Teodora the Nun, written in verse with a historical setting, is also significant in that it anticipates the next and best-known phase of Marquina's theatrical career, his historical drama. In addition, Malvina and don Diego are prototypes of many of the author's future protagonists, including especially don Diego's namesake in *The Sun Has Set in Flanders*. In 1944 Marquina acknowledged the importance of *Teodora the Nun*: "As the play has come down to us, my interest is still aroused by seeing delineated in it, struggling to take form, — accompanied by the stumbling of the mass of cerebralisms that overcame me at the time — the idea of my future verse theater" (*Works*, I, 1235).

VI Mala cabeza (Ne'er-do-well)

In 1906 Marquina staged what was for him a rather different type of play. In *Ne'er-do-well*, a brief work in three parts, the author studies the domestic problems of a comfortable, middle-class family of "our times," that is, 1906.[8]

"Mala cabeza" is Antonio, the Simón family's younger son, who, from his parents' point of view, can't do anything right (especially when compared to his older brother, the mother's favorite). Antonio knows his mother is adulterous and attempts to prevent her meeting with her lover. The father discovers the truth and decides to leave his wife and older son. Antonio, now suddenly "grown up," departs with his father and a faithful maid, Pacorra.

In *Ne'er-do-well*, Marquina is concerned with the dual problems of adultery and the transition from adolescence to young manhood. Neither theme is fully developed, due to the brevity of the play, within whose limits Marquina has trouble operating. The drama is important in that it is an early example of the author's "contemporary" plays, the major part of his dramatic production during the years 1915–1920.

VII   Benvenuto Cellini

Marquina's last major play to reach the stage bafore his success with *The Daughters of the Cid* was *Benvenuto Cellini.* Produced in 1906, the play is essentially structured around four incidents extracted from Cellini's *Vita.* Marquina's major departure from the autobiography is the creation of Escorpina, the woman Cellini grows to love and who does not exist in the original. Acts I and II take place in Rome, with Cellini first an apprentice and then a master artist. The third acts finds him in the service of François I in France. In the last act Cellini in Florence breaks with the Duke of Cosme over the interpretation of a statue of Perseus. The Duke wants the artist to represent the sovereign triumphing over the will of the people. With the help of the poor in Florence, Cellini finishes his version which shows the "spirit of the age" that crushes all usurpation and force.

In *Benvenuto Cellini*, the dramatist exalts the value of art above all utilitarian principles and the right of the artist to create freely. Marquina as a struggling young author more than likely sensed a parallel between Cellini's life and his own. Marquina's protagonist, who also appears in one of his stories, *El reverso de la medalla (The Other Side of the Medal),* follows in general the autobiographical portrait. The playwright has maintained Cellini's characteristic arrogance and self-assurance but has imbued him with a more noble and democratic nature. This change in Cellini's character, his finding moral and material support among the poor of Florence, and his desire to "make from art . . . things as common as bread for all" shed some light on a concept contained in the play but not formalized (*Works*, I, 411). Although the theme is a secondary one, Marquina is expressing an idea with Socialist overtones: the democratization of art. This concept is reminiscent of views held by the

Englishman William Morris, whose writings were popular at the turn of the century.

Escorpina symbolizes Marquina's idealized concept of the role of the woman in a man's life. She is Cellini's source of inspiration and is at his side during every crisis. Escorpina denotes a major step in the development of the author's female protagonists, whose idealized characteristics are visible in his first plays but not clearly delineated until *Benvenuto Cellini*. Throughout Marquina's dramatic career, the author shows a marked preference for this concept which carries him toward "an ideal woman, each time more concrete — the woman as a mother."[9]

In *Benvenuto Cellini* "Marquina begins to show definite signs of mastering dramatic technique. His character portrayal is more convincing. . . . There are more threads of interest and intrigue, without distraction from the main ideas, woven into the plot."[10] The critical reception was rather favorable, and the play managed to last ten days. One reviewer stated that in *"The Sheperd* the 'dramatist' peeked out behind the poet's somewhat deliberate nebulosities. In *Benvenuto Cellini* he boldly stood forth."[11]

The staging of *Benvenuto Cellini* placed Eduardo Marquina on the threshold of his first theatrical success. In these early works, Marquina served his initial dramatic apprenticeship. Some of Marquina's more important themes make their appearance, such as the exaltation of "good" love over "bad" and the idealization of the female figure. Two of the author's main types of plays are anticipated: historical and rural dramas. The only principal category not yet included is Marquina's religious dramas. The author still shows a preference for prose works. Only *The Shepherd* and *Teodora the Nun* are in verse. There is still insufficient mastery of dramatic technique, and the plays have no clear-cut conflict raising and development.

In general, these plays lack organic unity, as Marquina is unable to reach a synthesis of the various dramatic components. The author has not been able to create dramatic dialogue characteristic of the person speaking, particularly in the rural plays written in prose. In the verse plays, excessive rhetoric and lyricism diminish the theatrical effect, and character delineation is still weak.

Marquina's early plays clearly show that the dramatist was undergoing a period of experimentation. On an ideological plane the au-

thor had not yet adopted the conservative stance that would characterize his dramaturgy starting in 1908. Two of the pieces, *The
Shepherd* and *The Dauphin*, reflect the author's youthful "rebellious" spirit. In *Benvenuto Cellini*, the author expounds an idea with
a socialistic character: the democratization of art; while in *Teodora
the Nun*, Marquina faces contemporary Spain, at least in the play's
initial conception, from a "regenerative" and "Europeanization"
point of view. The other plays written during this period deal with
more conventional themes and seem to give no indication of the
author's sociopolitical concerns.

CHAPTER 3

Historical Theater I: Revival of "Poetic Theater"

I Introduction

ON March 5, 1908, Eduardo Marquina scored his first significant
theatrical success with the première of *Las hijas del Cid* (*The
Daughters of the Cid*). During the six years that had elapsed since
the unsuccessful staging of his first play, *The Shepherd* in 1902,
Spanish theater had undergone a significant change.

In 1902, José Echegaray, the dominant figure of the Spanish stage
during the last third of the nineteenth century, and who was to
receive the Nobel Prize in 1904, was still a dramatic force to be
reckoned with. However, by 1908 his melodramatic and artificial
plays of honor had largely fallen by the wayside, to be replaced for
all practical purposes by the plays of Jacinto Benavente whose low-
keyed and antirhetorical theater was the antithesis of Echegaray's.
Benavente, the "father" of Spain's modern theater, built upon late
nineteenth-century plays by such authors as Enrique Gaspar and
Benito Pérez Galdós who had vainly attempted to establish alterna-
tives to the melodramas of Echegaray.

The year 1908 saw the continued success of Carlos Arniches and
the team of the brothers Joaquín and Serafín Alvarez Quintero,
playwrights who had established themselves toward the end of the
nineteenth century as the major exponents of Spain's comic theater.
As we have indicated in our study of Marquina's early dramas, the
plays written by Benavente and his followers on the one hand and
by those who continued in the fashion of Arniches and the Quinteros
on the other, came to represent two of the three main currents of
Spanish theater during the first part of the twentieth century. The
third was represented by verse drama, the so-called "poetic the-

ater," whose re-appearance on the Spanish stage stems initially from
the successful première of Marquina's *The Daughters of the Cid*.[1]
Although the poetic theater did not gain the wide popularity enjoyed by the other two kinds of theater, it did achieve a certain
measure of success, and many authors, some quite noteworthy,
followed the path of Marquina.

Verse had been the usual form of written dramatic expression
since the earliest known beginnings of Spanish dramaturgy and had
managed to survive the inroads of prose until the middle of the
nineteenth century. After the effervescence of the Romantic theater
had run its course and Realism had begun to manifest its influence,
plays written in prose made their appearance in some of the works
by dramatists such as Adelardo López de Ayala and Manuel Tamayo
y Baus. However, verse was the medium utilized by Echegaray, and
his dominant position breathed new life into verse drama. Eventually, Echegaray himself felt the influence of prose, and from 1885
onward his theater shows a preference for this form of dramatic
expression. The rise of Benavente's theater, which was entirely in
prose, forced original verse plays off the Spanish stage, although
occasional new productions of Classical and Romantic Spanish plays
managed to keep verse drama tenuously before the public eye. It
was in this void that Eduardo Marquina successfully premièred his
verse play *The Daughters of the Cid*.

The dramatist quickly backed up his new-found popularity with
two consecutive successes, *Doña María la Brava* (*Doña María the
Intrepid*) and *En Flandes se ha puesto el sol* (*The Sun Has Set in
Flanders*), staged in 1909 and 1910 respectively and both written in
verse. The many authors who followed the way opened by Marquina
assured a renaissance of verse drama in twentieth-century Spanish
theater. The period 1910–1920 witnessed verse plays by, among
others, Ramón del Valle-Inclán, Enrique López Alarcón, Francisco
Villaespesa, Ramón de Godoy, Fernando López Martín and Ramón
Goy de Silva. During the 1920's the brothers Antonio and Manuel
Machado and Federico García Lorca also wrote plays in verse, along
with Luis Fernández Ardavín and Joaquín Montaner.[2] The poetic
theater flourished during these two decades, 1910–1930, gradually
diminishing thereafter. After 1930, a few authors such as José María
Pemán and Agustín de Foxá; and at times Rafael Alberti and Miguel
Hernández also wrote verse drama. However, the genre never
again reached the popularity of the period 1910–1930. Today, as was

the case at the beginning of the century, verse drama on the Spanish stage is essentially limited to occasional performances of Golden Age plays and to the annual production of José Zorrilla's *Don Juan Tenorio* around All Saints Day in November.

The poetic theater in twentieth-century Spain is characterized, particularly in the decade 1910–1920, by the historical setting of a great many of its plays.[3] In general the historical plays produced during this period did not view Spain's past with a critical eye. Instead of guiding the spectator toward an evaluation of the historical problems that weighed upon him as a Spaniard, these works carried him to a remote past devoid of any vital connection with the present. The authors attempted to continue the tradition of seventeenth-century Spanish drama, but it is obvious that too often they were closer to the excesses of the Romantic theater than to the Golden Age. Although the poetic theater produced a series of fine plays, on many occasions, particularly during the decade 1910–1920, its authors allowed themselves to be influenced by the more exaggerated and affected aspects of the Romantic theater, so that at times their plays resembled a caricature of the dramatic tradition they were attempting to continue. Marquina's historical dramas written during the years immediately following his initial success with *The Daughters of the Cid* reflect some of these excesses. However, his plays are superior to the general run of verse dramas written during this period by authors such as Francisco Villaespesa. Marquina was soon to recognize what he has called the "affectation" afflicting both his own historical dramas and the poetic theater in general, and he stopped writing verse plays between 1916 and 1919 in favor of a series of prose plays with a contemporary setting (*Works*, III, 1351).

The novelist Ramón Pérez de Ayala included a parody of the poetic theater of the day in his *roman a clèf, Troteras y danzaderas (Mummers and Dancers)*, published in 1913. One of the novel's characters, the poet Teófilo Pajares, stages a ridiculous verse play dealing with the tragic love of Liliana de Rousillon and the troubadour Raymond de Ventadour. Between the acts, a certain don Alberto del Monte-Valdés — apparently Valle-Inclán disguised — severely criticizes the play's obvious faults.

The critics have not been able to determine who Pérez de Ayala had in mind when he created Teófilo Pajares, although both Francisco Villaespesa and Eduardo Marquina are prominently mentioned. Angel Valbuena Prat has pointed out several metrical similarities between Pajares' play and Marquina's *The Sun Has Set in Flanders* but admits that "the subject as well as many of the details of the play invented by Ayala recall, above all, Villaespesa's theater. . . ."[4] José García Mercadal in his edition of *Mummers and Dancers* leans toward the Villaespesa theory, whereas Andrés Amorós in his detailed study of Pérez de Ayala's novel identifies Pajares as Marquina.[5] Neither critic, however, offers conclusive proof.

The Marquina theory seems rather difficult to believe in the light of the letters written by Pérez de Ayala to the author of *The Sun Has Set in Flanders* precisely during the period of *Mummers and Dancers'* publication.[6] In various letters the novelist requested free tickets from Marquina, whose brother-in-law was then the director of a theater in Madrid. Though these letters, of course, do not eliminate Marquina as a possible candidate, it is hardly likely that Pérez de Ayala would have dared to request complimentary tickets from a dramatist he had so satirized and ridiculed.

The poetic theater came under fire five years later in 1918, when Pedro Muñoz Seca staged his "historical" play in verse, *La venganza de don Mendo (Don Mendo's Revenge)*, a work in which he parodied the affectation of the verse drama then in fashion. More recently, Gonzalo Torrente Ballester has strongly criticized the poetic theater. However, at the same time he has pointed out certain of its positive aspects as evidenced by the following comment on Muñoz Seca's parody: "The satirist's good fortune succeeds in caricaturizing the deteriorated and declamatory forms of said theater, but perhaps without attempting it, he carries along and envelops in the satire the noble values that the poetic theater tried to maintain: the chivalresque sense of life, loyalty, honor, and sacrifice."[7]

II *Marquina's Historical Plays*

When Marquina staged his plays during the years 1908–1910, he was able to take advantage of a situation in Spain that favored the type of theater he was producing. The dramatist started his career soon after Spain's disastrous war of 1898 with the United States. Once the defeated country's initial depression had lessened, there was a patriotic awakening that emphasized the positive and focused on the extolling of Spain's virtues. Among the many examples of this love of country, there is the "return to the subject of history, projected on a heroic scale, within whose climate triumph the first plays of the Marquina of 1906 *(The Daughters of the Cid)*."[8]

The reaction against Realism and the subsequent lyric character that impregnated literature toward the end of the nineteenth century also facilitated the author's attempt to restore verse drama to the Spanish stage. All Hispanic literatures came under this lyrical influence, "even the least subjective genres, such as the theater and the novel."[9] This "departure from Realism" in the theater in Spain was not an isolated instance for "playwrights throughout Europe joined the revolt."[10]

Marquina's early success was also helped by the active support he received from María Guerrero and Fernando de Mendoza who headed Spain's most renowned theater company of the day. During an association that began with the première of *The Daughters of the Cid* and lasted until María Guerrero's death in 1928, the company staged many of Marquina's dramas, some of which were written expressly for this actress, perhaps the major figure on the Spanish stage during the first part of the twentieth century.

Marquina's historical plays are the most abundant in his dramatic production, covering a period of more than forty years, from *Emporium* written in Catalan at the turn of the century, to his last play to reach the stage *El galeón y el milagro (The Galleon and the Miracle)* in 1946. Marquina shows a marked preference for setting his historical plays — practically all of which take place in Spain — in a period that covers the second part of the fifteenth century and the following sixteenth and seventeenth centuries. In other words, the span is from the last years of Juan II in Castille — *Doña María la brava (Doña María the Intrepid)* — to the times of Philip IV — *Por los pecados del rey (For the King's Sins)*. There are, of course, exceptions, among them *The Daughters of the Cid*, set in the eleventh century. Although the following outline does not include all the possible variations offered by Marquina's historical dramas, it does provide an overview of the different focuses the author gives to his individual plays:

A. *Historical figures as protagonists:* Well-known figures out of Spain's past have the main roles, i.e., the Cid, the Catholic monarchs and Gonzalo de Córdoba, although events and

characterization may not necessarily have historical validity.
Plays of this nature are *The Daughters of the Cid, Las flores
de Aragón (The Flowers of Aragón)* and *El Gran Capitán
(The Great Captain)*.
B. *Historical events with fictional characters in the main roles:*
The author freely follows the general outline of history, but
the characters are products of his imagination, as in *The Sun
Has Set in Flanders*.
C. *A historical setting without direct references to actual events
and characters in Spain's past:* The author limits himself to
creating a costume drama and allows his imagination free
rein to create characters in Spain's past, for example in *El
retablo de Agrellano (The Altarpiece of Agrellano)*.

The three historical plays *The Daughters of the Cid, Doña María
the Intrepid,* and *The Sun Has Set in Flanders* mark a change in the
playwright's ideology. Marquina, in the prologue prepared for the
publication of his complete works, discusses with some detail his
break with the sociopolitical ideas of his youth. In that prologue,
written in 1944 during the post-civil war period in Spain when all
ideas alien to the regime were suspect, the dramatist makes a con-
certed effort to disassociate himself from the radicalism of his youth.
He describes this early period of his life as his "temporal stigma"
and "original sin" all of which disappeared when he "found himself"
(*Works*, I, vii–xvi). Starting in 1908 Marquina adopted a traditionalist, conservative point of view and identified with the "establishment" in Spain. This change was permanent and is clearly
reflected in both his theater and poetry.

III   Las hijas del Cid (The Daughters of the Cid)

The play is set toward the end of the eleventh century when the
Cid is lord of Valencia. In accordance with King Alfonso's request, a
wedding has been arranged between the Cid's daughters, doña Sol
and doña Elvira and the Infantes of Carrión. The cowardly Infantes,
finding Valencia and the Cid's men hardly to their liking, decide to
leave for Galicia. In the oak woods of Corpes the Infantes become
drunk and each attempts to make love to the other's wife, leaving
the girls, as seen in the next scene, with their clothing in shreds and

bloodstained. When the Cid arrives, Elvira asks that one of the men accompany her to avenge the dishonor.

In the last act, the Cid, who has returned to Valencia, is informed that in the court held by King Alfonso, Téllez Muñoz — who is secretly in love with doña Sol — has killed the Infante Diego and that a mysterious adversary has killed Fernando. Messages arrive asking the daughters in marriage for the Kings of Aragón and Navarre. The mysterious adversary is really Elvira who returns badly wounded from the duel with the Infante Fernando. Elvira dies shortly thereafter, and as the play ends the Cid exclaims: "Kings, fatal destiny of my house!/Go back, go back, or return my daughter to me!/No, they don't listen to me . . . , they are coming!/I hear them entering . . ./(*Works*, I, 624). Marquina adds the following stage directions which allude to the play's implied tragic aspirations: "The kings appear at the door, dressed in armor, wearing their helmets, impenetrable like a final destiny. The tragic scene keeps them from going farther" (*Works*, I, 624).

In *The Daughters of the Cid*, Marquina has attempted to meet some of the traditional conventions of tragedy such as the "elevated" language of poetry, the "upper-class" status of its characters, and the fatal ennobling death of the victim. Yet only in Act IV and partly in V, which is the last act, does he succeed in creating a tragic climate, while Acts I–III are unnecessarily long expositions. However, an overview of the play reveals that Marquina's dramatic technique had improved, especially from the point of view of the poet's making more concessions to the dramatist during the six years that had elapsed since his initial première.

The source of *The Daughters of the Cid* is the epic poem, *Mio Cid*. Marquina tells us that as he read the verses dealing with the dishonor in the oak woods he was deeply moved by the exclamation: "If only Mio Cid Campeador would now appear!" The playwright felt the drama contained in these words as he imagined the Cid's reaction faced with his daughters' misfortune and soon thereafter wrote *The Daughters of the Cid*.[11] "One of Marquina's merits," states Ramón Menéndez Pidal referring to this play, "consists in having been the first dramatist to directly take as a model the original *Poem of Mio Cid*, forgotten since the eighteenth century in a quantity of rehashings and copies, each time farther removed from the original."[12]

The play reflects the patriotic spirit of the day mentioned in the introduction to this chapter. Marquina dedicated *The Daughters of the Cid* to the "new life of the heroes who died with love and pain for old Castille" and "to the future of the mother country" (*Works*, I, 501).[13] Manuel Bueno in his review of the première singled out this patriotic spirit as he attempted to explain the play's success: "In the play the shadow of a hard and chivalresque past is evoked that, be it historical or legendary, could not help but make our people proud."[14]

Marquina made considerable changes in the material offered by the epic poem. The play is constructed around the daughters' dishonor in the oak woods and has as its general outline the events leading from the time of the Cid's reign in Valencia to the request for the daughters in marriage by the Infantes of Navarre and Aragón which ends the epic poem. Some of Marquina's more notable changes are: The relatively great amount of space allowed to the Cid's stay in Valencia, the expanded role played by the Infantes — including a budding plot with the Moors of Valencia — the amplification of the scene in the oak woods, the frustrated love between doña Sol and Téllez Muñoz, the elimination "on stage" of the court held by Alfonso, the vengeance carried out by Elvira, and the death of the Infantes of Carrión who are simply defeated in a trial by combat in the epic poem.

The major and most daring variation was to change the focus from a well-known historical figure like the Cid to his daughters, who are poorly delineated in the epic poem. Marquina's Cid has lost much of the aura of the epic hero, although the play's last scene is an exception. Ramón Menéndez Pidal praised *The Daughters of the Cid* in general terms, but criticized the playwright's elimination of the "major scene" — the court held in Toledo where the Cid obtains justice for the dishonor in the oak woods. He particularly censured Marquina's interpretation of the epic poem's hero: "He is presented as a hero who after having forged his destiny as he wished, upon finding himself without strength, allows himself to be possessed by the mania of marrying his daughters to kings, and when he is successful, loses his head. . . . This Cid is too far removed from the equanimity always shown by the Cid in the ancient poem, who, far from desiring a marriage with high nobility, only accepts it when imposed by his sovereign, in the first marriage as well as the second."[15]

In defense of Marquina's characterization we must keep in mind that essentially, he was expanding upon traits already in the epic poem, where the Cid appears as a devoted father and husband. If we can break away from the inevitable comparison with the original, Marquina's Cid is able to stand alone as a credible character. Moreover, the Cid in Marquina's play is only a secondary, albeit important character, as the dramatist is primarily concerned with the daughters.

In Marquina's early plays, we have noted the author's preference for the observation of feminine psychology, frequently focusing his attention on two women, one "good" and the other "evil." In *The Daughters of the Cid* another pair appears that we find in later plays: two women, one "strong" (Elvira), the other "weak" (Sol). Marquina characterizes her in the work's opening line when the Cid's wife, doña Jimena, states: "Sol, my daughter, you will always be a little girl . . ." (*Works*, I, 505). Doña Sol's drama is twofold, since besides suffering dishonor, she also loves Téllez Muñoz. Sol's struggle is between her filial love and sense of sacrifice on the one hand, and the love she feels for Téllez Muñoz on the other. Marquina does not reveal Elvira's character immediately as he does with doña Sol, and initially we have no inkling of her true nature. Her character is clearly defined, however, in the oak woods when the two sisters feel threatened by the Infantes and Elvira vigorously exclaims: "Alone with them and the road is dark,/bloodthirsty ideas boil within me!" (*Works*, I, 579). Toward the end of the play, Marquina sums up his conception of Elvira's character when doña Sol exclaims: "She and my father had the same spirit." Although Menéndez Pidal found praise for the general conception of the daughters, he noted that their "characterization is overly elementary, contrasting one with the other."[16]

Marquina has not given any depth to the Infantes of Carrión and has limited their delineation to a series of negative characteristics: cowards, traitors, liars, etc. Yet in Marquina's conception of the play their role is important, since their very presence is intended to charge the work with a menacing air of tragic destiny. The Cid's wife has a limited role, as does don Jerónimo, the archbishop of Valencia. Among the secondary characters, Téllez Muñoz is the most credible. His most dramatic moment comes in the oak woods when he approaches doña Sol after the dishonor.

Compared with future works produced by the poetic theater, *The*

Daughters of the Cid is a relatively sober play, in which the osten-
tatious display of the author's ability as a versifier is kept at a
minimum. Marquina has also been able to imbue the play with a
vigorous spirit reminiscent of the epic poem. *The Daughters of the
Cid* was more an artistic than monetary success. It lasted from
March 5 to March 20, 1908. However, the Spanish Royal Academy,
ignoring the box-office receipts, awarded Marquina the Piquer Prize
for dramatic excellence. More importantly, the play helped to establish Marquina as a playwright of note and initiated the renaissance of
verse drama on the Spanish stage.

IV   Doña María la brava (Doña María the Intrepid)

The following year, 1909, Marquina continued to use Spain's past
as source material and premièred the "dramatic ballad," *Doña
María the Intrepid*. The play is set in the fifteenth century during
the last years of the turbulent reign of Juan II. Alonso Pérez de
Vivero, in order to help his prince, Enrique — the future Enrique
IV — has killed don Alonso, son of the widow doña María. Enrique, in love with doña María, has attempted to take away from
Alonso a small jewel containing her picture. In the ensuing struggle
Alonso is killed. María suspects her archenemy, don Alvaro de
Luna. Don Alvaro, who is also in love with doña María, finally
succeeds in convincing her that he is not the murderer. Enrique,
finding himself alone with doña María confesses that Vivero is
guilty. María seizes her son's sword and kills Vivero. Don Alvaro
takes the blame to save doña María, and although she admits her
guilt, no one believes her. Finding herself alone with don Alvaro,
she finally realizes that she loves him. The play ends with don
Alvaro on his way to the gallows.

In *Doña María the Intrepid* the dramatist follows the patriotic
vein observed in *The Daughters of the Cid*. Marquina dedicates the
play "to the ancient idea of justice, exaltation, passion, and glory of
our nobles and our plebeians who have engendered, aggrandized,
fixed, and perpetuated the Castilian race . . ." (*Works*, I, 627).[17]
Doña María is a symbol of Castile, representing the spirit of justice
and patriotism cited in the dedication. Alongside this patriotic
theme, Marquina develops one of his favorite subjects: the observation and analysis of the female psyche. Doña María is a phase in the

evolution of a type of strong and deeply moral woman that appears in Marquina's theater, and whose first significant incarnation is Elvira in *The Daughters of the Cid*.

Amidst the corrupt atmosphere of the court of Juan II, María knows that she personally must avenge her son's death: "I shall do this myself./ I am not fooled by the justice of a court/that makes a farce of everything" (*Works*, I, 671). The play's conflict stems both from her desire for vengeance and the repressed love she feels for don Alvaro, whom she believes to be her son's murderer. Doña María is largely a product of Marquina's imagination, although apparently he had a historical figure in mind: "*Doña María the Intrepid*, one of the author's favorite works, . . . has as a foundation the heroic greatness of doña María de Pacheco, widow of the *comunero* Juan de Padilla, at the defense of Toledo."[18]

Marquina's major departure from Spain's history in his conception of don Alvaro is the imaginary love between the king's favorite and doña María. Having don Alvaro take the blame for Vivero's death has some historical basis, since according to the chronicles the latter was killed at the former's command.[19] The picture Marquina offers of this controversial figure out of Spain's past is rather favorable: intelligent, at times sarcastic, of a noble spirit, capable of the greatest sacrifice because of his love for doña María, and completely in control of himself, although one forms the impression that for reasons of state he would be capable of carrying out the most violent actions. Marquina characterizes the future Enrique IV by giving particular emphasis to his reputed rather sickly nature and bizarre personality. The prince's love for doña María is yet another product of the author's imagination.

Marquina wrote *Doña María the Intrepid* with greater care and thoroughness than *The Daughters of the Cid*, and thus expected greater success than with the previous play.[20] This creative effort is particularly evident in the relatively complete delineation of the protagonist, and in the elaborate stage directions, designed to create a medieval setting appropriate to the times of Juan II of Castile. However, in spite of the author's greater effort, *Doña María the Intrepid*, although well received, was not as successful as *The Daughters of the Cid*. The reviews were generally favorable but somewhat reserved.

The play did allow Marquina, however, to continue to improve his dramatic technique. Eduardo Gómez de Baquero recognized the

author's evident progress and stated that "one notices in the play a
certain ability to search for effects and situations that absorb and
move the spectator. It is not merely the work of a poet who has
given dramatic form to a poem and triumphs due to rhyme and
images. There is in the drama a revelation of the dramatist's specific
qualities and visible progress, with respect to *The Daughters of the
Cid*, in theatrical technique, particularly in bringing the action together and the joining of its parts."[21]

V   En Flandes se ha puesto el sol (The Sun Has Set in Flanders)

The Sun Has Set in Flanders was staged first in Montevideo on
July 27, 1910 and had its Spanish première in Madrid, December 18
of the same year.[22] The genesis of the play stems from a request
made at the beginning of 1910 by Fernando Díaz de Mendoza, who
asked Marquina for a new work to include in the Guerrero-Mendoza
company's repertory for its planned spring tour of Latin America.[23]

As in Marquina's two previous plays, *The Sun Has Set in Flanders*
has a double dedication. The first is to María Guerrero and Fernando Díaz de Mendoza. In the second, the dramatist maintains the
same patriotic spirit we have observed in *The Daughters of the Cid*
and *Doña María the Intrepid*: "To the memory of the generous dead
who far from Mother Spain have cold and forgotten graves, to renew
in them a conscious tribute of honor and piety, I write this canto"
(*Works*, I, 799). The Wars of Liberation in the Low Countries during
the seventeenth century provide the background upon which Marquina, making liberal use of "dramatic license" has based his play:

> Marquina has focused the entire period of the Wars of Liberation within the
> few years covered by the action of the drama. He has reproduced the
> background of the period without regard for the historical sequence of its
> events. He has not hesitated to use the most evident anachronisms. He is
> interested not in political or military campaigns, but in the fundamental
> differences in the character of two nations. For this reason his work, in spite
> of its inaccuracies, can claim a real historical value, since it represents fairly
> and sympathetically the spirit and the ideals of both the Netherlander and
> the Spaniard.[24]

The plot, following an act-by-act breakdown, is as follows:
Act I: The play opens in the home of the Flemish painter Juan
Pablo — in the Brabant region, between Antwerp and Mechlin.

The artist, his wife María Berkey, daughter Magdalena, and servant Groninga are anxiously speaking of the Spaniards who are sacking the region. Mander, who loves Magdalena but is not loved in return, arrives and states that he is leaving for Holland where their princes are gathering troops. As Magdalena speaks with her sister Clara, it becomes clear that the former is strongly attracted by the Spaniards. Shortly thereafter, a Spanish officer, Valdés, arrives with the wounded captain of his regiment, don Diego de Acuña. Weakly, don Diego announces that a peace has been negotiated and that he only seeks a spot where he can recover. Don Diego, fulfilling a condition of the peace treaty, orders his troops to depart for Italy. Once alone, Diego asks the Flemish to leave him, whereupon Magdalena inquires why their presence bothers him. The Spaniard answers directly: "Because tomorrow I shall love you, my lady!" (*Works*, I, 836).

Act II: The play continues in a fenced area back of don Diego's house near Antwerp. We learn through a conversation between two servants, Potter and Groninga, that the peace has not lasted. Juan Pablo is attempting to raise troops against the Spaniards, whereas don Diego, who has been promoted to the Council of Justice, pursues the rebels. Diego and Magdalena have married and have a son, Albertino. A group of peasants arrives seeking protection, and after a brief internal struggle, Magdalena hides them in her house. Juan Pablo and Mander enter and also are given refuge. Troops arrive searching for Juan Pablo, but before they can carry out their mission, don Diego enters, tears up the arrest order, and surrenders himself as prisoner in place of the Flemish, who are free to go. The act ends with the play's most famous line as Diego says to Magdalena: "Spain and I are like that, my lady!" (*Works*, I, 870).

Act III: Act III takes place in a house in the outskirts of Mechlin. Spain has suffered a series of defeats, and Mander with a few men has been able to free don Diego from prison. Juan Pablo has stopped fighting and has returned to his painting. Don Diego has lost his spirit and is a shell of his former self. However, his regiment returns from Italy, and although he attempts to resist their urgings, he finally leaves to join the Spanish troops.

Act IV: This act has the same setting as Act II. The Flemish have finally defeated the Spaniards. Bonfires are set to celebrate the victory. All, with the exception of Mander, understand don Diego's feelings and are compassionate. Diego returns, demoralized and resentful. However, Magdalena's affection and tenderness begin to have their effect and Diego slowly softens. His son Albertino will light a bonfire. However, it will not be to celebrate a victory, but rather to bring happiness. The play ends with don Diego and Magdalena joined in an embrace, shedding tears of joy as Albertino runs off to light the bonfire.

The Sun Has Set in Flanders is not the drama of Diego and Magdalena but rather the symbolic representation of the conflict between the Spanish and European spirit. Although the following description of the play's opposing viewpoints is exaggerated, it does synthesize Marquina's intent: "On the one hand, we have the Flemish with their cows, their printing press, their paintings, their books; their ideals are wealth, industry, comfort, enlightenment, and liberty. On the other hand we have the Spaniards with their swords, their pride, their generosity, and their faith; their ideals are honor, love, fame, and valor."[25]

The above conflict, couched in human terms, is initiated at the end of the first act when Diego exclaims: "Because tomorrow I shall love you, my lady!" (*Works*, I, 836). When Diego and Magdalena, who represent Spain and Flanders respectively, marry, circumstances force them on various occasions to live the personal drama of deciding in favor of love or country. Only Spain's final defeat will put an end to the couple's anguish. The sun sets on the Spanish empire in Flanders, thus initiating the eventual breakup whose last significant loss was the "Disaster of 1898," just twelve years before the play was written. However, Marquina's vision of Spain's defeat in Flanders is not somber. On the contrary, he extols the virtues of the Spanish people: nobleness of spirit, stoicism, pride, ideals of honor, generosity, sense of sacrifice, courtesy and faith, all of which gain in stature in the face of Spain's adversity. The Spaniards might have lost, but these virtues are constant and able to turn defeat into "victory." Marquina sums up this point at the end of the play when Magdalena attempts to encourage her demoralized husband. She tells Diego that although "despairing and defeated" his spirit is such that he has succeeded in bringing joy to all upon his return. Diego is really "victorious" for as Magdalena informs him: "The same who conquered you/by your greatness have been conquered . . ." (*Works*, I, 931).

This concept of Spain in the face of defeat is related to a similar viewpoint held by other writers of the period whose work was influenced by the war of 1898. Gonzalo Torrente Ballester has singled out this aspect of *The Sun Has Set in Flanders* which has generally been overlooked by the critics: "From a reading of this play we can deduce, without any great exegetical effort, that Spain has been defeated; but also that, Spain having fallen, the Spaniard will always have his personal virtues, the virtues of the Spanish people. . . . If one reads Unamuno attentively, it can be seen that the coincidence of thought is exact. In fact, the men of '98 believed for a good while not in the salvation of Spain as a collective entity, but rather in Spaniards as singular men."[26]

After the war of 1898 the subject of "Europeanization" became popular and was one of the solutions proposed to the so-called "problem of Spain." The dramatist had dealt with this subject in one of his early plays, *Teodora the Nun*, written in 1905. In *The Sun Has Set in Flanders* Marquina offers his vision of a new Spain that would evolve from the union of Spanish and European cultures and whose symbolic representation in the play is Albertino. "Just as in his son's hands don Diego's sword is turned into a torch, the Spaniards in whose spirit coexist the two previously contradictory cultures, will create the mother country of tomorrow, not with swords, but rather with torches of science, art, and poetry."[27] Yet Marquina in the play does not really adopt a critical attitude toward Spain's past and contemporary history. There is a greater emphasis on don Diego as a singular individual, of whom the postwar audience in 1910 could be proud, than there is on the need for the new Spain envisioned by Marquina.

Don Diego de Acuña, the dramatic embodiment of Spanish virtues, draws a self-portrait in Act I as he bids his troops goodbye: "If someone asks,/it would be good to answer/that, a Spaniard through and through,/I loved, fought, gave my blood,/thought little, prayed a great deal,/gambled well, lost quite a bit,/and because it was a mad undertaking. . . . I did not want to leave this world/without setting my pike in Flanders" (*Works*, I, 833). The impression don Diego gives in the play corresponds only in general terms to his conventional and cliché-filled self-portrait. His actions do not reveal all the characteristics he attributes to himself, some of which are worthier of a Don Juan adventurer than the altruistic individual presented by Marquina. This disparity is more than likely due to the probability that don Diego de Acuña is based on a previous don Diego, the nefarious donjuanesque protagonist in *Teodora the Nun*, who is the prototype of many of Marquina's male heroes in his historical

dramas, all of whom gain in moral character over the original. Don
Diego de Acuña is just too good to be credible; his many grand
entrances and gallant, sweeping gestures are simply overdone.

Magdalena is also based on previous models. She, like Escorpina
in *Benvenuto Cellini,* represents Marquina's idealized concept of a
woman not as a lover but rather "the woman as a mother." Magdalena's conflict is the same as don Diego's; she finds herself forced
to choose between her love for the Spaniard and her patriotism. Her
most difficult moment is the arrival of Flemish peasants seeking
refuge. They symbolize the Flanders who calls on her in time of
need. When Magdalena's sister, Isabel Clara, asks who they are,
one answers: "I am Flanders;/I am pursued and ask your protection . . ." (*Works,* I, 852). Marquina generally wrote his more important roles for women. However, in *The Sun Has Set in Flanders,*
there seems to be an equitable division. Don Diego takes the lead in
the first two acts, while Magdalena dominates the last two. This
dramatization of the couple's human conflict made a direct emo-
tional appeal to the 1910 audience, more than likely contributing to
the play's success.

With the exception of Juan Pablo, who finds himself torn between
his fervent patriotism and the growing affection he feels for his
son-in-law, the other characters are poorly developed. Isabel Clara
and Magdalena's mother are sketchily drawn, as is Albertino. Isabel
Clara represents the continuation in Marquina's theater of the
fragile, easily frightened young woman called doña Sol in *The
Daughters of the Cid* and who appears in many of the author's future
plays: "Poor little Isabel Clara/life frightens her/and she doesn't dare
enjoy it" (*Works,* I, 844). Mander is a static character and the only
"villain" in the play, since both Spaniards and Flemish are portrayed sympathetically. His flat, unchanging role consists essentially
of increasing Magdalena's anguish by appearing every so often and
reproaching her for her marriage to a Spaniard.

The Sun Has Set in Flanders reveals that the dramatist was beginning to drift away from the sober, relatively controlled treatment
achieved in *The Daughters of the Cid* toward the "affectation" Marquina himself has described as afflicting the poetic theater around
1916 (*Works,* III, 1351). The play suffers from the author's overabundant versification. All too often Marquina allows himself to be carried away by his lyric inspiration. These lyrical excesses are characteristic of many plays produced by Spain's twentieth-century poetic

theater. Even García Lorca is guilty of them in his historical verse drama *Mariana Pineda*.[28] In these plays, "The poet — like the librettist or the musician — stops the plot's progress in order to concentrate, in a fragment developed at the expense of the drama, his imagination, his elegiac, descriptive or other aptitude, but always with . . . an extradramatic lyric quality."[29] Two examples of this type of poetic "aria" in *The Sun Has Set in Flanders* are the long description of the new-born calves and the war ballad recited by Magdalena, both in Act I. It must be kept in mind that Spanish theater at the time functioned under the "star system." Theatrical companies were headed by a well-known actor or actress, and all was geared to the enhancement of the "star." Odd poems within a play could serve a double function. On the one hand the dramatist could attempt to dazzle the audience with his poetic talent and thus, if necessary, be able to cover up some of the play's defects, while the "star" could have a unique opportunity to dominate the stage. Such concessions to convention could not help but weaken the play's dramatic content.

In *The Sun Has Set in Flanders* Marquina has not successfully fused the play's elements into a theatrical whole. The work lacks structural firmness, and the author again has not fully bridged the gap between lyric poet and dramatist. Marquina himself did not expect *The Sun Has Set in Flanders* to be a success. In July of 1910 he wrote Díaz de Mendoza, who was already in South America, asking him to delay the play's première. The dramatist feared that he had written the work too hastily and that another of his dramas *El rostro del ideal (A Certain Face)* was a better play. As Marquina tells us, the letter arrived late, and the première of *The Sun Has Set in Flanders* in Montevideo was an "unequivocal success" (*Works*, I, 1238). To date *A Certain Face* has never been staged and justifiably so; it is clearly inferior to *The Sun Has Set in Flanders*. The Madrid première five months later in December, 1910 was again a triumph. Marquina was awarded the Piquer Prize for a second time — the first had been for *The Daughters of the Cid* — by the Royal Spanish Academy.

The Sun Has Set in Flanders was Marquina's first big success and is even today his most famous work. This notoriety explains, perhaps, the generalized erroneous tendency to describe the author's dramatic production in terms of *The Sun Has Set in Flanders*, in spite of the fact that Marquina wrote many vastly superior plays, particularly his rural and religious dramas such as *The Hermitage, the Fountain, and the River* and *Teresa de Jesús* respectively. Marquina, as a dramatic craftsman, developed far beyond the still relatively fledgling playwright of 1910. The author himself recognized his long apprenticeship in the theater when in 1924 he successfully premièred his rural drama *The Poor Little Carpenter:* "Here for the first time, it seemed to me that I was sure of my footing on the stage, twenty-three years after choosing the profession with the hendecasyllables of *The Shepherd* and sixteen years after entering it with the success of *The Daughters of the Cid*" (*Works*, III, 1355).

The Sun Has Set in Flanders, favored by the historical circumstances outlined, definitely established Marquina on the Spanish stage and helped to assure the renaissance of Spain's twentieth-century poetic theater. In an anonymous interview published in 1945, answering a question as to the significance of his dramatic production, Marquina noted: "These are things that one cannot or should not say. But since you have asked and I have to answer something, I'll tell you that I believe I have contributed to the resuscitation of verse theater which had been abandoned, and perhaps to the love of subjects distinctly Spanish."[30]

CHAPTER 4

Historical Theater II:
Success and Affectation

I Introduction

BETWEEN 1910 and 1916, Marquina continued to write histori- cal theater in verse, but none of the plays produced during this period attained the success gained by *The Daughters of the Cid* and *The Sun Has Set in Flanders.* Many defects that had begun to ap- pear in the latter play became clearly visible in *El Gran Capitán (The Great Captain)* staged in 1916, the year in which Marquina aban- doned historical verse drama and wrote a series of prose plays with a contemporary setting. The hiatus was to last until 1920 when he again wrote a historical verse drama, *Ebora.*

This step backward for the author's dramatic craftsmanship was described by Marquina in later years as the "affectation" of his theater (*Works,* III, 1351). However, in spite of the manifest "affecta- tion" in some of the plays, there is also an obvious effort by the dramatist to expand the limits of his historical theater, particularly in two humorous one-act plays *El antifaz (The Mask)* and *El gavilán de la espada (The Armed Hawk),* and also in *El retablo de Agrellano (The Altarpiece of Agrellano)* in which Marquina uses witchcraft as source material. In the plays of this period, 1910–1916, the poet still maintains an advantage over the dramatist. Marquina has not yet completely purged his theater of those lyrical bursts, truly "arias," that obstruct the play's development. Characterization is still weak, and none of the figures created by Marquina are comparable to his protagonists in *The Hermitage, the Fountain, and the River* and *María the Widow.*

After *The Sun Has Set in Flanders,* Marquina briefly interrupted

51

his series of plays inspired by Spain's history to write two works with a troubador setting, *El rostro del ideal (A Certain Face)* and *El último día (The Last Day)*. Around this time, 1911–1913, he composed the trilogy *Pasos y trabajos de Santa Teresa (Trials and Tribulations of Saint Theresa)* and the contemporary play in prose *Cuando florezcan los rosales (When the Roses Bloom)*.

II *Two Humorous Plays*

The dramatist returned to his historical series with the two previously mentioned one-act plays, *The Mask* and *The Armed Hawk*. Marquina has indicated that both plays reflect his effort to avoid "affectation" and to "open new paths" for his theater (*Works*, III,1351). These two plays, because they are humorous, are unique within Marquina's dramatic production. Only in *Rosa de Francia (A French Rose)*, written in collaboration with Luis Fernández Ardavín, does humor again appear.

Both *The Mask* and *The Armed Hawk* are delightful and full of life, and it is obvious that Marquina is enjoying himself. *The Mask* takes place during the time of Philip IV. Doña Clara, who is in love with the reluctant suitor don Lope, searches him out at a masked ball and enticingly feigns she is someone else. Don Lope intrigued by the mysterious masked lady, declares his love for her but soon thereafter discovers it is really Clara in disguise. *The Armed Hawk*, set in the eighteenth century, is more ambitious in its satirical intent, poking fun at those young ladies who can only fall in love with a man who matches up to their chimeric, romantic notions. Gonzalo, disguised as a bandit, kidnaps his cousin Estrella when she attempts to run away from home to avoid marrying him. Naturally her amorous interest is quickened by the bandit and all goes well.

Both plays have only two characters and were probably written with the famous actors Fernando Díaz de Mendoza and María Guerrero in mind. These plays have been ignored by the critics and have remained buried in Marquina's prolific dramatic production. They are interesting, however, in that they indicate that Marquina had the potential to develop a refreshing and light but satirical theater.

III   Por los pecados del rey (For the King's Sins)

In 1913 Marquina premièred *Por los pecados del rey (For the King's Sins)*, a historical verse drama in which he continues to make free use of the material offered by Spain's past. In *For the King's Sins*, as in his other historical plays, Marquina is not interested in the reconstruction of a period, but rather in capturing the spirit of the times within which he develops his dramatic fiction. In his dedication to Philip IV, the author indicates that the inspirational source of the work is that king's portrait by Velázquez — one of the dramatist's favorite painters. Marquina goes beyond historical facts, attempting to capture the king's "tragedy" that Velázquez could not paint for it "was not visible" (*Works*, II, 303). Velázquez' influence in the play is also evident in the appearance of various figures out of his paintings, i.e., "las meninas." The use of plastic effects is one of the basic dramatic techniques used by Marquina in his historical plays. He accumulates on stage many different characters, who with their varied and colorful costumes please the spectator's eye.

The play centers around the king's fruitless efforts to seduce María Candado, a young Castilian woman. The work abounds in palace intrigues carried out by the Conde Duque de Olivares, bent on maintaining his position as the king's favorite. However, the loss of Portugal is the catalyst that causes the Conde Duque to be dismissed.[1] The king, a solitary, pathetic figure, finally recognizes the error of his ways and desists in his attempts to seduce María.

Marquina's interpretation generally follows the historical outline of the figure of Philip IV. In the play he is a weak-willed monarch dominated by his favorite. The dramatist's hand is seen in the transformation of the king into a "good person" when he finally breaks with Olivares. The Conde Duque exhibits many of the sinister qualities attributed to him by history and legend. However, when he is dismissed, Marquina softens his dark portrait and gives the Conde Duque an air of dignity. In spite of the degrading atmosphere of Philip IV's court during the period when Spain loses Portugal, Marquina's habitual optimism and faith in the virtues of the Spanish people manifest themselves in María Condado.

This beautiful, intelligent, and virtuous country girl who is a symbol of Castile, not only resists the king's advances but attempts to save him from himself. Marquina underlines her symbolic role

when María, face to face with the king, censures Philip's illusions of
"maintaining the kingdom's greatness/throughout Europe and
beyond." The Marqués de Maqueda thereupon tells the monarch:
"The kingdom speaks with her voice" (*Works*, II, 343). Previously
María had criticized her father for attempting to gain favor from the
king by displaying a flag won in Holland: "We expect yesterday's
glories to bear fruit." She also adds: "I believe that among the
troubles/of the times, the worst/is to desire that yesterday's glories/
produce today's bread" (*Works*, II, 323–25). It is interesting to
observe Marquina's critical outlook in the words of María Condado
which could have had special meaning for those post-1898 Spaniards
who continued to see Spain in grandiose terms. Unfortunately the
author did not choose to develop his historical theater in this
direction.

After 1908 Marquina consistently extolled the virtues of Spain and
her people. It is likely for this reason that there exists the erroneous
popular notion that Marquina includes in his historical theater only
glorious moments of Spain's past. Enrique IV in *Doña María the
Intrepid* and Philip IV are far from glorious figures. *For the King's
Sins* and *The Sun Has Set in Flanders* include two setbacks from
Spain's history: the losses of Portugal and Flanders respectively.
Regardless of the period, however, Marquina in his historical plays
generally manages to sing the praises of Spain and her people. In
Doña María the Intrepid, next to Enrique IV we have the positive
figure of the protagonist who is the symbol of Castile; María
Candado in *For the King's Sins* has a role similar to doña María, and
in *The Sun Has Set in Flanders*, don Diego symbolizes Marquina's
concept of the Spaniard's singular virtues.

IV   El retablo de Agrellano (The Altarpiece of Agrellano)

In 1913 Marquina varied considerably the focus of his historical
theater in *The Altarpiece of Agrellano* which was based on an earlier
version written in 1910, *Cuento de una boda y desafío del diablo
(Story of a Wedding and the Challenge of the Devil)*. "Witches —
the   superstitions   dealing   with   witches — constitute   the
background or historical material of this drama" (*Works*, II, 1320).
Although the play takes place at the "beginning of the Spanish
Renaissance during the reign of Charles V," Marquina does not

otherwise use historical figures or events. The plot is extremely complicated and difficult to follow. Cordalia, violated by the Morisco don Lope, gives birth to a child, Verbena. Through the sorcery of don Lope's wife, La Gaifera, and the help of the humanlike Devil — called Aleppo in the play — who comes to life from his place on the altarpiece, — the Morisco is burned in his castle. Fifteen years pass. Verbena has fallen in love with the young painter don Felix. Aleppo, who has come to love Cordalia, kidnaps Verbena. Cordalia, in order to avoid harm to her daughter, accedes to Aleppo's advances. Don Felix kills Aleppo who "returns" to the altarpiece. Cordalia dies on Verbena's wedding day, thus fulfilling a prophecy that she would die on the day her happiness began.

The above summary is only a bare outline of the plot. However, it does serve to show how radically Marquina's thematic material had changed within the same year (1913) that saw the staging of *For the King's Sins*. Unfortunately, the dramatist lacked the experience to handle the play's complicated structure and subject. Previously he had written plays more or less following the standard pattern of introduction, complication, and resolution. The plays were intended to be logical and chronological and always functioned on one level. In *The Altarpiece of Agrellano*, the author had a difficult task before him with the multiple levels of meaning and the play between reality and fantasy, revolving around the theme of witchcraft. If Marquina had attempted this work during the 1920's, after more extended apprenticeship in the theater, he would not have encountered such difficulties.

Marquina reacted to "the opinion of many" who said the play was "murky" and added extensive explanatory notes when the drama was published in 1914, subsequently included in his complete works (*Works*, II, 1319–44). The dramatist defends his interpretation, stating that he wished to observe the Devil from three different points of view: first from a "Catholic idea of a personal Devil," second as seen by "men of the Renaissance, who denied the existence of witches, laughed at them, and also denied the Devil's existence," and last — the dramatist's own original point of view — the Devil seen through "Cordalia's soul and character" (*Works*, II, 1322–23). This multiple view, according to Marquina, did not allow the play's development to be logical. The notes do clear up many points and in themselves are quite interesting for their revelation of the author's creative process.

V   Two One-Act Plays

Marquina interrupted his series of historical dramas in 1914 to write *La hiedra (Ivy)*, a prose play with a contemporary setting. In his next historical work, *Cantiga de serrana (Mountain Song)*, also written in 1914 and never staged, Marquina moves away again from the more political theater represented by plays such as *The Sun Has Set in Flanders* and *For the King's Sins* and finds his source material in Spain's literary past. The play draws both on the Archpriest of Hita's *Libro de buen amor (The Book of Good Love)* and the mountain songs written by the Marqués de Santillana (*Works*, II, 784–85). The protagonist, Gadea de Riofrío, whom Marquina borrows from the Archpriest of Hita, is led on by the traveler, Pero Gómez, with false promises of marriage. When Gadea is abandoned by Pero, she commits suicide. This type of play is not repeated by Marquina and remains an isolated effort to vary and expand the limits of his historical drama. It is worth noting, however, that Marquina's interest in Spain's early poets is shared by other writers of the period: "The Generation of 1898 . . . attempts to revive primitive poets (Berceo, Juan Ruiz, Santillana). . . ."[2]

Within the same year (1914) Marquina completed the one-act "lyric drama," *La morisca (The Morisca)*. The work takes place around 1490 before the fall of Granada when "the racial aversion that crystalized in the so-called 'expulsion of the Moriscos' was beginning to take hold among the people" (*Works*, II, 804). Marquina views the past plight of the Moriscos with compassion and dedicates the play to them. This racial theme is focused on the impossible love between the Morisca Mari-Cruz and the Spaniard, don Alonso. The latter's overwhelming concern with maintaining "purity of blood" is the obstacle that does not allow him to declare his love. Mari-Cruz, who has converted to Christianity, symbolizes the plight of converts in Spain, rejected by both Moslems and Christians: "Alone and hopeless!/I am neither of Castile, nor of Granada!/I have no land other than my poorly dug grave" (*Works*, II, 827).

VI   Las flores de Aragón (The Flowers of Aragón)

Marquina's third play in 1914 was *The Flowers of Aragón* which has as its historical framework the royal wedding between Isabella of

Castile and Ferdinand of Aragón. The drama's plot consists of a number of episodes dealing with the obstacles that Ferdinand and Isabella had to overcome before marrying. Between the two protagonists Marquina has a marked preference for the future Catholic Queen, who appears again in his next historical play, *The Great Captain* and in one of his novels, *La reina mujer (The Queen is a Woman, Too)*. Although the playwright incorporates into Isabella's personality many of the characteristics attributed to her by historians, i.e., astuteness, intelligence, and decisiveness, among other traits, he is essentially concerned with creating a woman in love who wishes to marry for that reason and not for reasons of state. In this respect, Isabella is one more of the many women in Marquina's theater who to reach true love must overcome a series of obstacles. Although the author's conception of Ferdinand is rather harsh in *The Great Captain*, this is not so in *The Flowers of Aragón*. In the latter work, Ferdinand is brave and quickwitted, although also stubborn, particularly in his dealings with the Castilian nobles. He is also in love, but not to the degree of passion reached by Isabella.

The Flowers of Aragón was only moderately successful. A reviewer of the play's première stated that "the audience did not show that spontaneity nor that generous applause with which on other occasions it has shown its satisfaction."[3] *The Flowers of Aragón* is a relatively well written and structured play, not overburdened by the "affectation" mentioned previously. However, except for introducing the subject of the Catholic monarchs, the story was not very original within Marquina's dramatic production. If the play had been staged just a few years before, around 1910 when the public was more receptive to this type of theater, it would have enjoyed greater success.

VII   El Gran Capitán (The Great Captain)

It became clear that Marquina's historical theater was beginning to lose its appeal when the première of *The Great Captain* on March 30, 1916 was given an "icy reception" by the audience.[4] The play's run lasted only eleven days. The author, who dedicated *The Great Captain* to its protagonist, has stated that he wished to "give in theatrical form a personal and poetic impression of Gonzalo de

Córdoba's soul and the times in which he lived."[5] The play revolves
around the impossible love of don Gonzalo for the Catholic Queen,
Isabella, whose influence is the sole motive of his actions in the first
two acts. He is either defending the Queen's honor or covering up
the King's infidelities so that Isabella will not suffer. Act III consists
of a series of palace intrigues which mistakenly lead Ferdinand to
believe that don Gonzalo wants to make himself king of the Spanish
possessions in Italy. Don Gonzalo is called back from Italy but
manages to prove his innocence. The Queen, who does feel an
attraction for don Gonzalo, orders him to return to Italy. As the play
ends, the protagonist sadly admits to himself that he will never see
the Queen again.

Marquina's conception of don Gonzalo is totally idealized. His
personality consists of a series of positive characteristics. He is kind,
brave, faithful, intelligent, altruistic, and, of course, in love with
Isabella. In short, he is too good to be true. This very personal
conception was severly criticized. Constancio Eguía Ruiz has
observed that in the play we do not see Gonzalo de Córdoba as the
hero he really was, but rather as a "fervent page in love with the
Queen, who is always subject to her will and who considers love the
only stimulus to his undertakings."[6] Although the above statement
is somewhat exaggerated, it is essentially valid. We find in Gonzalo,
amplified and on a different level, basically the same type of
"Spanish" virtues that the dramatist attributed to don Diego in *The
Sun Has Set in Flanders.*

Marquina's characterization of Queen Isabella is less daring.
Although he indicates adequately that Isabella loves Gonzalo, the
playwright does not allow this feeling to surface clearly. With the
exception of this repressed sentiment, Marquina's delineation of
Isabella corresponds fairly closely to the historical figure. Ferdinand
pales by comparison with the exalted don Gonzalo. The Catholic
King appears very suspicious of those who might threaten his
power, particularly in his dealings with don Gonzalo. Marquina
emphasizes especially his involvement in intrigues, the tension
between him and Isabella, and his marital infidelity. Marquina's
Ferdinand is far from being a fool, but next to Gonzalo he comes out
second best.

The play is dominated more by Marquina the poet than by
Marquina the dramatist, a fact not missed by the critics. The
author's overabundant versification is particularly evident in

Isabella's long praise of the Alhambra which interrupts the work's dramatic development. The author did not soon forget the criticism to which *The Great Captain* was subject, both in its performance and in its subsequent publication (*Works*, II, 1355). When his complete works were published in 1944, Marquina included extensive notes in which he attempted to justify his interpretation of the play's historical background (*Works*, II, 1344–56). These defend his position, emphasizing the play's subtitle, "Legend of Chivalresque Love" and poetic license, both of which Marquina feels allowed him a certain latitude in his interpretation. He also quotes a series of works to support his version.

After the play's unsuccessful staging, Marquina perceived what was happening to his theater and stopped writing historical plays and using verse until 1920. *The Great Captain* closes an important period of Marquina's theater. Today it is his most famous period, although as we have pointed out, it does not include his best plays. During the rest of his life, Marquina wrote some historical verse plays, but these were relatively few and spanned a period of thirty years.

CHAPTER 5

Historical Theater III: Last Plays

I *Introduction*

THE year 1916 was decisive for Eduardo Marquina. As we have seen, his last two historical dramas had clearly shown that the type of theater he was writing, inspired by Spain's past, had begun to lose its audience appeal. The author's earlier efforts to expand the limits of his historical drama with plays such as *The Mask, The Armed Hawk, The Altarpiece of Agrellano* and *Mountain Song*, had not significantly influenced the direction of his theatrical production. In the notes included in his complete works that pertain to his "tragedy" *Ebora* written in 1920, Marquina makes a series of retrospective observations on the type of historical verse theater written during the first quarter of the century.

Beginning with the première of *The Daughters of the Cid*, and especially after the success of *The Sun Has Set in Flanders*, verse theater, which had been neglected since the decline of Romanticism, gained new strength. Each year, with works of varying fortune, some excellent and successful, this or that poet tried his luck, enriching the repertory. . . . But all of us, I don't know how, without thinking, and as if by instinct had confined ourselves prematurely as we wrote these plays . . . between unnecessary partitions of a kind of historic brickwork that limited poetic invention and caused the theatergoing public sudden indigestion brought on by monotony. We forget, perhaps, the fertile variety of human themes, — vital, realistic, fabled, or authentic, — that was characteristic of our Classic or Baroque theater; in short, "Spanish," if we are to give it its natural, unmistakable, and legitimate name, (*Works*, III, 1351)

Faced with the above perspective, Marquina decided to change the focus of his theater: "Finally, vexed, and in order to escape from an affectation that could reach a point of no return, I gave up verse for some years. I was in America for eleven months, met other audiences and new Spains, and I allowed the postwar climate to penetrate within me and saturate me with its changing themes in a series of prose plays" (*Works*, II, 1351–52). The "some years" Marquina refers to are 1916 to 1920, that is from the première of *The Great Captain* to the writing of his historical drama *Ebora*: "I returned to verse with *Ebora*, attempting to draw away at least in time and in the very style, from the accustomed historical mode that pained me to wear out. . . . The success of *Ebora* reconciled me to verse. I was not to abandon it again in a systematic manner. Likewise, and for the same reason, I reaffirmed my determination to open new paths that could help us avoid a possible stiffness, traveling through history as through our real world. Living it more and declaiming it less" (*Works*, III, 1352).[1]

Although Marquina did attempt to reform his historical dramas, the new works did not attain the success previously enjoyed by his plays of the years 1908–1910. After a concentrated effort to revive the genre between 1920 and 1923, Marquina wrote historical plays only intermittently.[2] However, this attempt at reform brought the dramatist to the realization of the importance of controlling his verse. Starting in 1920 there is an obvious toning down of the declamatory verses so characteristic of his previous plays. The poet Marquina was learning to write dramatic verse and to eliminate his lyrical outbursts.

II   Ebora

The three historical plays Marquina wrote immediately after his return to verse are *Ebora*, *Rosa de Francia* (*A French Rose*), and *Una noche en Venecia* (*A Night in Venice*). In each, the dramatist made an attempt to change the focus of his historical theater. In *Ebora*, true to his stated desire of drawing away from the "accustomed" mode of his historical theater both in time and style, Marquina sets his play in the Iberian peninsula during the Roman occupation. *Ebora*, subtitled "Tragedy in a Prologue and Three Acts," deals with the destructive passion of Ebora, Queen of Cantabria, to inculcate in her grandson's soul the same hate that she holds for the youth's mother, the Roman Lucia Liciana. All her efforts are fruitless as Marquina shows us that bonds between mother and child, regardless of the circumstances, are unbreakable. When Ebora learns that she has failed, she commits suicide.

The play's major innovation is the author's effort to create a tragedy within an early historical framework, not usual in his theater. In addition, there is a definite toning down of his declamatory verses, clearly setting this play apart from his previous historical drama, *The Great Captain*. The protagonist, Ebora, is another in the line of Marquina's strong, energetic heroines, such as Elvira and doña María in *The Daughters of the Cid* and *Doña María the Intrepid*, respectively. The characterization of Lucia Liciana as a woman of rather loose morals is unique in Marquina's theater, since the dramatist usually tends to idealize his mother figures. Marquina also attempted to increase the relevancy of his historical theater by incorporating into the play's dramatic texture the tenor of the times in post-World War I Europe. The dramatist stated that there "palpitates in *Ebora* the foreboding of a possible threatening tomorrow, following a war that has not been able to extinguish nor overcome hate among men" (*Works*, III, 1352).

III   Rosa de Francia (A French Rose)

In 1921 Marquina varied again the character of his historical drama when he sought the collaboration of the playwright, Luis Fernández Ardavín, for the composition of *Rosa de Francia* (*A French Rose*). Marquina had not co-authored a play since 1904 when he wrote *El delfín* (*The Dauphin*) with José Salmerón. In the notes that accompany his complete works Marquina has explained why he decided to work with Ardavín: "Each day I became increasingly determined to react against possible affectation by inserting in the framework of the versification of historical material the vital charm of a 'human' episode, of human relations between men and women. I searched for the subject by myself and then proposed to Ardavín . . . that we should collaborate on *A French Rose*." (*Works*, III, 1353).

The historical framework of the play is the reign of Philip V, when the monarch (married to Isabel de Farnesio), abdicated in 1724 in favor of his son, Luis. The reign of Luis I, who was married to Luisa Isabel of Orléans, — Marquina's French rose — ended after six months when the young king died of smallpox. Marquina and

Ardavín drew freely on this historical material and made their play revolve around the rivalry between Isabel de Farnesio, who was noted for her intrigues, and Luisa Isabel. The play consists of a series of related humorous episodes in which Isabel de Farnesio attempts to keep Luis I separated from his French wife, in the belief that she can thus better dominate the young king. In the end, of course, love and Luisa Isabel triumph.

The play has a delightful freshness about it, and it is obvious that both dramatists are enjoying themselves. Marquina tells us that the joint effort was "in reality a literary exercise, free and enjoyable, that neither of us will forget" (*Works*, III, 1354). *A French Rose* recalls those Spanish Golden Age plays such as Calderón's *La dama duende* (*The Phantom Lady*) that are structured around complicated comic plots which involve the characters in equivocal situations leading to misunderstanding. Marquina and Ardavín are firmly in control of the play and keep the action moving quickly forward. *A French Rose* and Marquina's two humorous one-act plays *The Mask* and *The Armed Hawk* show that he had a definite talent in this direction which he did not continue to exploit.

IV   Una noche en Venecia (A Night in Venice)

A French Rose, written in 1921, did not reach the stage until 1923, the same year that saw the première of Marquina's next historical play, the "dramatic poem," *Una noche en Venecia* (*A Night in Venice*). This play is devoid of concrete historical references and set in a mysterious, vaporous, and ethereal Venice. Such change in Marquina's theater could have served a double purpose. First, the play's "atmosphere" could have allowed his poetic muse freer rein, as opposed to the relatively realistic settings of his previous historical plays, which required a more sober, less lyrical versification. Second, the omission of concrete references to the past could have put him out of range of those critics who censured the lack of historical veracity in his plays. Marquina had already written a play with an ethereal setting the previous year (1922) — *El pavo real* (*The Peacock*).[3] However, in *A Night in Venice*, it is not a case of exotic oriental legends as in the former play, but rather of a donjuanesque Spaniard in that Italian city. Don Pedro de Alcántara is another of Marquina's male protagonists related to that original donjuanesque type, don Diego, who appeared in *Teodora the Nun*. However, don Pedro offers one distinguishing and contradictory trait for a Don Juan: he promised his father on his deathbed to marry a certain woman and have nothing to do with other women. Although this woman died on the eve of the wedding, don Pedro, who finds himself in Venice, is faithful to his promise. Two women, Sara, the Jewess, who is goodness incarnate, and Laura, the prostitute, compete for don Pedro's love. As always in Marquina's theater, goodness triumphs. The dramatist adds an additional dimension, as he is also interested in showing the redemptive power of love which succeeds in converting Laura into a "good" person.

Marquina's major innovation is the play's ethereal atmosphere, alluded to by its subtitle, "Poetic Drama." Although the author has succeeded in creating a poetic climate, he has paid limited attention (perhaps purposely in over-dependence on mood), to such dramatic requirements as characterization and structure. The critic Enrique de Mesa found praise for *A Night in Venice*, not so much as a play but rather as a "staged poem."[4]

A Night in Venice represents a marked innovation within Marquina's historical theater. However, the author apparently did not consider this type of play a viable alternative, since he did not again write a work of this nature. *Ebora*, *A French Rose*, and *A Night in Venice* constitute Marquina's last concentrated efforts at historical theater. During the 1920's he changed the focus of his dramatic production and created a series of excellent rural plays.

During the balance of his theatrical career Marquina wrote historical dramas only on occasion. While these last historical works are generally well constructed — *El galeón y el milagro* (*The Galleon and the Miracle*) is an exception — and exemplify Marquina's mature ability as a dramatic craftsman, none reached the success of the plays of 1908–1910, nor significantly influenced the direction of his theatrical production. In the remainder of this chapter we will summarize only the more significant aspects of these last historical plays.

V   En el nombre del padre (In the Name of the Father)

En el nombre del padre (*In the Name of the Father*) did not appear until 1935, twelve years after the première of *A Night in Venice*.[5]

For the first time, Marquina sets a play on the South American continent, specifically in colonial Peru. The plot deals with the conflict between the rich Spaniard, Fernán Bustos, and his illegitimate son Bustillos, born of the Inca doña Solís. Marquina shows that blood ties are stronger than existing differences as father and son are finally reconciled. The author has stated that in the play there "beats in embryonic form the historical progress of the vast drama of Spain in America."[6] The work has as its symbolic antecedent *The Sun Has Set in Flanders*. In the earlier drama Diego and Magdalena represent Spain and Flanders respectively, while their son is the symbolic union of these two peoples. The same role is attributed to Bustillos, who is the symbol of the union of Spain and the people of Latin America.

VI   La bandera de San Martín (San Martín's Flag)

In 1937 while in exile in Buenos Aires, Marquina wrote two historical plays, *La bandera de San Martín* (*San Martín's Flag*) and *La Santa Hermandad* (*The Holy Brotherhood*). The first of these is a brief one-act play that revolves around the efforts of San Martín's wife, Remedios Escalada, and four other women to finish the flag of independence. During the length of the play the characters continuously extol liberty and independence. Liberator San Martín never appears, but his voice is heard at the end addressing his troops. Marquina has indicated that he also intended to write a play dealing with the meeting between San Martín and Bolívar that decided the future of the United Provinces (*Works*, V, 1180). This project, never carried out, is related to another play that Marquina had in mind just before his death, based on the life of the Viceroy of New Granada, Solís. Both unfinished projects, along with *In the Name of the Father*, *San Martín's Flag*, and one act of *The Galleon and the Miracle*, indicate that Marquina's historical interests in the last years of his life tended toward Latin America. This new direction was very likely influenced by his stay in Argentina during the Spanish Civil War.

VII   La Santa Hermandad (The Holy Brotherhood)

In *La Santa Hermandad* (*The Holy Brotherhood*), premièred in Santiago, Chile in May of 1937, Marquina traces a parallelism between the Spanish Civil War and the period of Ferdinand and Isabella when the Catholic monarchs, to achieve national unity, limited the power of the nobles and feudal lords. *The Holy Brotherhood*, which was originally a rural police established by the Catholic monarchs, is in Marquina's play the chief instrument of national unification. The opposing forces of the Spanish Civil War are symbolically portrayed in *The Holy Brotherhood* through the conflict of two brothers, one "good," Blas, and the other "bad," Martín, representing the Nationalist movement and the Republic, respectively. Marquina's sympathies are clearly with the Nationalist movement.

The Holy Brotherhood had the makings of an excellent play, which could have had profound meaning in 1937: the fratricidal confrontation of two opposing ways of understanding the nation's future. However, instead of exploring and penetrating below the surface of the problem, the dramatist resolves the confrontation in a simplistic manner in favor of one of the contending parties. It is interesting to note, however, that Marquina's inherent human goodness manifests itself clearly in this play. In 1937, in the midst of a bloody civil war, when cries for vengeance were ringing out on both sides, the dramatist in *The Holy Brotherhood* was asking for reconciliation among Spaniards, as both brothers are finally reunited.

VIII   El galeón y el milagro (The Galleon and the Miracle)

Marquina staged his last historical play, *The Galleon and the Miracle*, in 1946. This work seems to be a nostalgic return to those dramas of patriotic exaltation that Marquina wrote around 1908–1916. However, in *The Galleon and the Miracle* Marquina does not take himself as seriously as in the earlier historical dramas, as seen in the subtitle: "Romantic serial in five acts." The play is supercharged with the episodic adventures of the Spaniard Fonseca, who attacks pirate ships in the Indies and becomes a famous guerrilla against the French in the War of Independence. True to the subtitle, Marquina is more interested in maintaining action and suspense than in constructing a tight plot or creating credible characters.

Critical reaction to the play was rather good, ranging from the effusive opinion of Alfredo Marquerie to the reserved praise of Raimundo de los Reyes who added that the play "is not, by far, among the author's best works."[7] The play's success was helped by the fact that Spain's situation during the difficult postwar years was conducive to the escapist theater exemplified by *The Galleon and the Miracle*. The play is important within Marquina's dramatic production as his last work to reach the stage during his lifetime; it indicates that to the very end, he never really gave up the idea of writing historical drama.[8]

CHAPTER 6

Rural Plays

I *Introduction*

IN 1924 Marquina premièred his rural play *El pobrecito carpintero*
(*The Poor Little Carpenter*) and with it initiated the second
important category of his dramatic production.[1] Although most of
the author's early plays take place in a rural setting, they are only
the efforts of an aspiring dramatist, whereas *The Poor Little
Carpenter* is the "play that is able to mark the transformation of the
first Marquina to the second . . .", representing the author's theater
of "full maturity."[2] Unfortunately, Marquina's historical dramas are
so well known that the tendency is to overlook his rural plays,
including two of his major works, *The Poor Little Carpenter* and *La
ermita, la fuente y el Río* (*The Hermitage, the Fountain, and the
River*). Both these last are dramatically more effective than any of
his historical plays. Marquina has given his version as to why he
returned to rural drama after so many years: "It was necessary to
clear my concept of the Spanish *pueblo* of all its random and
contemporary diversity; of its intranscendental clamor for suffrage
and impersonal democracy and politics in order to contemplate the
rural people in their eternal innermost regions of natural wisdom
and inspired arts" (*Works*, III, 1357). This statement must be paired
with those made by the author dealing with his early plays as part of
his "original sin" (*Works*, I, x). In both statements the author is
referring to his youthful nonconformism that led him to write a rural
play like *The Shepherd* which contains an anarchistic ideology.

Between 1924 and 1932 he was to write six rural dramas, all in
verse. The author intended to incorporate what he called "modern
themes" into his rural dramas, yet the statement just cited suggests
he chose to ignore the recently increased social conscience of the

Spanish *pueblo*, manifested not only in rural areas but in the cities as well.[3]

The author's progress as a dramatist is evident in these plays. With a few notable exceptions, Marquina has given his rural theater a low-keyed, sober treatment. The setting is realistic, devoid of bucolic or Romantic concepts. There is a clear-cut conflict presentation, firmly carried toward its resolution. As Marquina's theater evolved, his dramatic verse became less affected and acquired a more natural air. In these rural plays, although on occasion the author will revert to bad habits, his verses are geared to dramatic function. Marquina situates most of his rural dramas in Castile, although others, such as *Fruto bendito (Blessed Fruit)* and *Fuente escondida (Hidden Spring)*, take place in the Pyrenees. Regardless of place names, the background of all these plays, apart from some minor allusions, is essentially the same.

Marquina has varied somewhat his favorite situation of two women who struggle for the love of the same man. In three plays *The Poor Little Carpenter*, *Salvadora*, and *Los Julianes (The Julianes)* the adversaries are men who vie for the same woman. Yet despite the familiar situation, the dramatic treatment in these rural dramas is far superior to that of previous plays. The one notable exception is *The Julianes*, a rather disjointed play that closes the series. As is generally the case in Marquina's theater, the important roles are for women, even in *The Poor Little Carpenter*, the title notwithstanding. In this series the study of the female psyche, which is one of the constants of Marquina's dramatic production, is skillfully transposed into theatrical terms.

II El pobrecito carpintero (The Poor Little Carpenter)

Marquina took an entire year to write *The Poor Little Carpenter*. This effort stands in marked contrast to the scant two months spent on *The Sun Has Set in Flanders*. The action takes place in a Spanish village in a region not identified by the dramatist although one reviewer felt it had a Catalan air.[4] José, the village carpenter, who lives with his sickly, eccentric younger sister, Susina, gives refuge in his home to the so-called "Abuela." The Widow Romero accuses the Abuela of having stolen firewood on her land and insists that José throw her out. When the carpenter refuses to do so, the widow, who knows that José and her step-daughter, Gracia, love each other, decides to arrange a marriage between the latter and Antoñón, the blacksmith. Antoñón realizes that his fiancée and José still love each other and challenges the carpenter to a fight later that evening. However, before the fight can start, Antoñón saves Susina, who, believing herself an obstacle to her brother's happiness, has attempted suicide. José and Antoñón become friends again, and with the latter's blessing, the former is reunited with Gracia. The Abuela arrives and with veiled allusions announces that the widow Romero has died in a fire. When the Abuela leaves, a cross is formed over the path she has taken. Susina in a feverish state cries out, for she is the only one to see the cross.

The apparent simpleness of this "village tale" is precisely what Marquina hoped to achieve: "*The Poor Little Carpenter* has been conceived and drawn in the spirit of these tales; it reproduces silhouettes of characters and themes of action that abound in them, and like them makes use of procedures of simplification and purification of reality, to make it more significant and give it values of poetic expression and poetic transcendency."[5] An essential feature of the play (which no plot summary can hope to reproduce) is the unique atmosphere created by Marquina.[6] Although the realistic setting predominates, the author has tinged it with an ethereal quality especially in the delineation of the Abuela, José, and his sister Susina. The play differs in this respect from the other rural dramas whose setting is realistic, with "flesh and blood characters." In *The Poor Little Carpenter*, the author has drawn a fine line in creating his characters. In a review of the play's opening, Enrique Díez-Canedo stated that "the true virtue of this drama consists . . . in the exactitude with which everything takes on body, we could almost say mortal flesh. . . . Marquina has dealt with his present characters as only a true poet can. He has given them the body necessary to live. That is, that his characters are made up of an almost musical substance."[7] José is good through and through, but faced with losing the woman he loves, besides his friend Antoñón, he regrets having been good and vows to change: "In this world one must first wound/in order to kiss later;/it is necessary to be good and bad/. . . to show your teeth, to alternate a caress with a club . . ." (*Works*, III,1024). As in a "folk tale," goodness will triumph over evil, and José, because he really does not change, regains both

Gracia and his friend. The Abuela summarizes the play's theme at the end when she says goodbye to the carpenter: "An appreciative debtor/I have already paid you for the water, fire, and bread/others stoned me and in their hide they shall carry/the mark of my wound,/good for good; evil for evil./ In this life,/what we give we get" (*Works*, III, 1069). Besides being Marquina's spokesman and a sort of fairy godmother to José, the Abuela serves as the stimulus that sparks the action and carries it to its conclusion. Although she is not on stage as much as José, the Abuela so dominates the play that the role of the carpenter pales somewhat. The Abuela and other old women that Marquina created to "do or say something good" are patterned in part on "Tita," a kindly maid in the Marquina household during the dramatist's childhood, who happened to be a distant relative of Goya.[8] The performance by María Guerrero in another of Marquina's plays, *The Altarpiece of Agrellano*, also influenced the conception of the Abuela and very likely explains the role's importance, since the dramatist wrote many dramas with the famous actress particularly in mind (*Works*, III, 1356–57). Gracia, who has a strong egotistical streak, is a notable exception to Marquina's usually idealized woman that triumphs in love. Susina is another of the author's young, frail, and impressionable heroines, such as doña Sol in *The Daughters of the Cid*.

The first two acts are the best of the four. Act I has a melancholy, lyrical air; Act II is more realistic and of strong dramatic impact. The third act, also rooted in everyday reality, fails to measure up to the second, while the last acquires some of the first act's "air" and finishes with Susina's mystical vision. The special "climate" that Marquina has given *The Poor Little Carpenter* points up one of the difficulties in arriving at a just evaluation of his plays. Today the tendency is to judge Marquina's theater on the basis of reading, with little or no attempt made to consider its original, ultimate destination, the stage. Although the play's dramatic virtues are evident, to judge by the newspaper reviews of its first performance, *The Poor Little Carpenter* has greater stage possibilities than can be discerned in a reading. Marquina's theater was conceived primarily as drama, not as literature, and only if this aspect of his work is kept in mind can we objectively judge his plays. Marquina has singled out *The Poor Little Carpenter* as a personal high point in his career as a playwright: "Here for the first time, it seemed to me that I was sure of my footing on the stage, twenty-three years after choosing the profession with the hendecasyllables of *The Shepherd* and sixteen years after entering it with the success of *The Daughters of the Cid*" (*Works*, III, 1355).

III   Fruto bendito (Blessed Fruit)

In 1927 Marquina premièred *Fruto bendito (Blessed Fruit)* a rural drama whose setting is the main house on a large land-holding in the Spanish Pyrenees. The theme is the maternal yearning of the protagonist, Andrea, daughter of the property owner, don Justo. Andrea has a suitor, don Abel, the village teacher, but she pays him scant attention. Dionisia, a maid in the household becomes pregnant, and Andrea decides to sacrifice everything and leave with the unmarried expectant mother. After thirteen months, Andrea returns with Dionisia's daughter and gives vent to her maternal instinct in her care of the child. When Dionisia returns to claim her daughter, Andrea and her parents attempt to keep the child. However, the child's father, Roldán appears and leaves with Dionisia and his daughter. Andrea and her parents are sad, but the experience has made her realize that she loves don Abel, the schoolmaster.

In *Blessed Fruit* Marquina develops a psychological study of Andrea's maternalistic yearnings. The protagonist's problem as seen by Marquina, who gradually reveals her personality in each of the three acts, is an aversion that she seems to feel toward love, both in its spiritual and physical aspects. She would like to be a mother without experiencing the biological process. The play's title is based on a line from the Hail Mary and reflects Andrea's attitude. In the second act, Andrea gives free rein to her desires and actually begins to feel as if she were the child's mother: "I love her as a daughter; maternity is something more than just flesh" (*Works*, III, 1296). Dionisia, who has a child out of wedlock and then lives as a prostitute before claiming her daughter, is the direct opposite of Andrea.

Although the play was well received, it did not achieve the success of *The Poor Little Carpenter*. *Blessed Fruit* is somewhat long, and in the third act Marquina shifts his focus abruptly to concentrate on Dionisia, leaving Andrea temporarily adrift. This play unfolds in a strictly realistic setting with no trace of the ethereal climate of *The Poor Little Carpenter*, which allowed verses more latitude. The result indicates that Marquina had not completely learned to adapt his free-wheeling dramatic verse to the realistic setting. Yet *Blessed Fruit* is an important play in that it served as a transitional link between *The Poor Little Carpenter* and *The Hermitage, the Fountain, and the River*, a play in which Marquina showed that he could maintain the poetic quality of his dramatic verse and adapt it to everyday rural reality.

IV   La ermita, la fuente y el río
(The Hermitage, the Fountain, and the River)

A month after the opening of *Blessed Fruit*, Marquina, on February 10, 1927 premièred *The Hermitage, the Fountain, and the River*. It is one of his best plays and ranks alongside his religious dramas, *Teresa de Jesús*, *The White Monk*, and *María the Widow*. Enrique Díez-Canedo in his review of the work indicated that "it was one of the best of all" of Marquina's dramas.[9] Just as *The Poor Little Carpenter* marked the playwright's transitional phase, *The Hermitage, the Fountain, and the River* is the drama that "could begin the complete maturity of Marquina's theater."[10] *The Hermitage, the Fountain, and the River* stands out among Marquina's theatrical production thanks to the strongly convincing delineation of its protagonist, Deseada; the dramatic, tragic climate that permeates the work; and the effective fusion of poetry and drama. The title corresponds to the play's three acts set at the three locations indicated: a hermitage, a fountain, and a river, which represent three symbolic stages in the psychological development of the protagonist. Marquina maintains his play in a realistic setting with no indication of the ethereal climate characteristic of *The Poor Little Carpenter*.

In the first act Deseada laments to her friends, doña Flor and Basilea, in front of the hermitage that she is already thirty years old and has lived all her life without love. Deseada has a suitor, don Lorenzo, who is about fifty years old, but she doesn't seem to be very interested in him. Although Deseada had an opportunity to marry when she was younger, she preferred to sacrifice herself and care for her younger sister, Lucía. Her sister is now a young lady and has a twenty-one-year-old fiancé, Manuel. The priest, don

Anselmo, notices the attraction she feels for her sister's fiancé and warns her of the danger. However, that very day Deseada finds herself alone, face to face with Manuel who, on an impulse, takes her face in his hands and kisses her passionately.

During Act II, Deseada remains in the background, while the focus shifts to the malicious gossipers. These form a kind of Greek chorus which congregates around the village fountain and comments on what has occurred, for Manuel has not remained silent. Unbeknownst to Deseada and Manuel, some of the gossipers arrange that they meet "by chance" in a store facing the fountain. Lorenzo's arrival incites Manuel to challenge him. Although Lorenzo tries to avoid a violent confrontation, since Manuel's grandfather had once saved his father's life, the two fight and the older man is wounded.

Act III takes place outside of a mill alongside a river. Lorenzo has not died thanks to the care of Deseada and Flor de Harina, the miller. Manuel, through Lorenzo's efforts, is to be released from prison, and although Deseada still loves him, she plans to leave the village so that the young couple can be happy. Her sister Lucía is not aware of the reason behind the fight. Deseada tells Lorenzo that it is enough that Manuel has loved her. If he belongs now to Lucía, he once belonged to her. However Deseada's world falls apart when Manuel returns and declares that he had fought only out of vanity and pride, not because of love. Deseada disappears behind the mill and drowns herself. That night Lorenzo, faithful to the last, watches over her body.

As in the case of *The Poor Little Carpenter*, a plot summary cannot capture the special atmosphere Marquina has given the play. Although the piece is written within realistic boundaries, *The Hermitage, the Fountain, and the River* is imbued with a tragic, melancholy air whose essence is encompassed in the following verses that Deseada delivers in the third act: "The hermitage, to begin/one morning to live/the fountain to suffer/and the river to cry" (*Works*, IV, 137). More than in any other previous play, Marquina has achieved the difficult union of drama and poetry. This is precisely one of the major problems of Marquina's theater, since the crucial fusion is not always achieved. Enrique de Mesa clearly makes this point when he indicates à propos *The Hermitage, the Fountain, and the River* that "the bard walks the tightrope that separates the dramatic poem from the lyrical poem. This is a nuance characteristic of Marquina, which gives him a personal inflection among the dramatists of his time, and which takes flight, if it is successful, and is shackled when not."[11]

The action of *The Hermitage, the Fountain, and the River* is essentially concentrated in Deseada. Even in Act II, when she stays in the background, her presence is felt among the gossipers around the fountain. Deseada, along with the protagonists of *Teresa de Jesús* and *María the Widow,* forms the triumvirate of Marquina's foremost dramatic characters. The theme in *The Hermitage, the Fountain, and the River* is the tragic frustration of Deseada's sensual instincts. Deseada, a symbolic name, means "desired." The young men in the village feel intuitively the crisis of this thirty-year-old woman, and all of them "desire" her, hence the name. One of the young men graphically describes her when he exclaims: "She passes . . . and as she passes/she burns the earth beneath her feet" (*Works*, IV, 67). From the very first scene in front of the hermitage, Marquina creates an aura of tragedy around Deseada, firmly maintained until the end of the play. The conflict is clearly presented in the moment that she kisses Manuel: her sexual desire sweeps her toward the young man, against the love and sense of obligation that she feels for her younger sister, Lucía. During the entire play, although racked with desire, she maintains her personal dignity and pride. It is only toward the end that Deseada begins to falter, and even then she is prepared to leave, despite loving the young man. For Deseada, before discovering the truth, it is enough that Manuel has loved her even though briefly: "Only one day of love/in my lifetime is enough./. . . My life is no longer night!" (*Works*, IV, 142).

Although Deseada dominates the play, Marquina has carefully drawn his other protagonist, Manuel. The young man is basically good and of a noble spirit, but with all the bravado of youth. He is anxious to prove his manliness, but lacks experience. Lucía, though adequately convincing, is based on previous models. She resembles the frail and impressionable young women who appear so often in Marquina's plays, of the same mold as doña Sol in *The Daughters of the Cid,* Susina in *The Poor Little Carpenter,* and Lolín in *When the Roses Bloom.*

Besides the main characters, various minor ones must be singled out, since they synthesize each of the play's acts. The priest, don Anselmo, is the concrete manifestation of the faith and hope symbolized by the hermitage in the first act. Two women, La Jueza and doña Quiteria, lead the gossipers in Act II near the fountain and are like the "chorus in the ancient tragedy who prepare catastrophes for the hypocritical pleasure of crying over them."[12] Flor de Harina, the stoic old miller whose daughter had accidentally drowned in the river many years before, summarizes in the third act the author's point of view. In answer to Lorenzo's query as to what he and his wife have taken in order to have lived so long in spite of all their sufferings, the old man indicates that the answer is "time . . . the river/of time that passes/and polishes and rounds/the rocks of pain" (Works, IV, 122). However, Lorenzo retorts: "But there are sharp rocks/that don't allow themselves to be rounded/ even by the rough buffeting of the river of time." Flor de Harina responds: "No; but those are the ones the river carries toward the sea" (Works, IV, 122). This conversation is a prelude to Deseada's suicide for she, like a rock that would not be rounded, is carried off by the river. Marquina calls for a reaction vis-à-vis life's suffering similar to that of Flor de Harina who affirms: "The greatest consolation I have is to know/that I was suffering pain and did not deserve it./ . . . I say/that in this world nothing is lost;/so that, if my pain were not punishment,/it probably was the advance payment/for another better life, and I bless it!" (Works, IV, 122).

V   Last Rural Plays

Marquina's next rural drama, Salvadora, was staged in 1929 and is set in Castile's Guadarrama Mountains. Again, the author concentrates the dramatic action in a female protagonist whose name the play bears. Jacobo Granda, "the master" (who wants to marry a rich woman so that he can pay his debts), has arranged a wedding between his mistress Salvadora and the apparently timid, middle-aged Tomé.[13] Jacobo, however, has no intention of abandoning his amorous relationship with Salvadora. The main body of the play concerns the protagonist's efforts to ward off Jacobo's advances and to convince Tomé of her wifely fidelity. The climax is reached in a face-to-face confrontation between Jacobo and Tomé, who has lost his timid demeanor. Just as Jacobo is about to stab Tomé, Salvadora reacts and kills her former lover.

The plot bears some resemblance to Terra baixa (Lowlands) written by the Catalan dramatist Angel Guimerá and premièred in 1897.

In *Lowlands* we find the same three main characters: the "master" Sebastián who attempts to maintain an ilicit relationship with his former mistress, Marta, after marrying her off to one of his laborers, Mannelich. It is quite possible that Guimerá's dramatic production might have influenced Marquina. Not only did the Catalan author write rural dramas, but he also composed historical verse plays, many of which were staged in Barcelona during Marquina's youth.

In *Salvadora*, Marquina extols the purifying force of matrimony that accomplishes the protagonist's transformation from "fallen woman" to faithful wife. Salvadora sums up this theme toward the end of the last act when, referring to her wedding day, she tells Tomé: "The dress of honor/that one day they put on me/mockingly, and which fit/so perfectly that, at once/it became part of my flesh and blood!" (*Works*, IV, 690). In general *Salvadora* evinces the technical progress evident in *The Poor Little Carpenter* and *The Hermitage, the Fountain, and the River*. Marquina has rooted his play in everyday reality, and his characters are closer to the earth than those in the plays just cited. In keeping with this setting, the dramatist has taken care to give his verse a natural air.

In *Fuente escondida* (*Hidden Spring*), staged in 1931, again the author focuses on a central female character, and in particular on one aspect of her personality. The protagonist, Nadala, attempts to repress her amorous sentiments, preferring to adopt the outwardly brusque, strong personality necessary in working her family's large farm, for which she is responsible. However, Nadala falls in love with the local Don Juan, Sintu, and eventually her true feelings appear, like a "hidden spring" reaching the surface. Among Marquina's heroines, Nadala is closest to Andrea in *Blessed Fruit*, both of whom try to repress certain sentiments to which they eventually give in. Andrea, in spite of her longings to be a mother, rejects all her sensual inclinations, while Nadala attempts to deny herself the fulfillment of the love she feels.

Hidden Spring reveals, however, as does *Salvadora*, Marquina's progressive development as a dramatic craftsman. This technical soundness was singled out by one of the play's reviewers who indicated that "from beginning to end, everything in the play follows a weighed and exact rhythm. . . . Nothing superfluous, nothing that signifies a roundabout manner. Each element has its exact importance; each character's participation corresponds to a need."[14]

This expertise is markedly diminished in Marquina's last rural drama, *Los Julianes* (*The Julianes*). The protagonist, Julián Julianes, a rural Don Juan has a child, Julianillo, by his mistress Fulgencia, and then abandons them to marry a wealthy woman, Jacoba. Fulgencia eventually marries Julián's half-brother, Juan, and the couple is blessed with three more children of their own. Julián and Jacoba have been unable to have children, and in contrast to the happiness of the other couple, lead a rather empty life. The situation is resolved by Julianillo's desire to work and live on his father's farm, thus bringing happiness to the childless couple.

The general construction of *The Julianes* would indicate that Marquina spent little effort on the play. The work is disjointed, as if the author simply added an epilogue to tie up loose ends and give the play a conventional happy ending. Marquina has tried to give more nearly equal importance to his main characters, perhaps shying away from his usual concentration of the dramatic action in a dominant female protagonist. The net result is that the characters are rather shallow.

Marquina himself apparently was not happy with the results, since *The Julianes*, which opened on May 13, 1932, was his last rural play, completing the cycle begun in 1902 with *The Shepherd*. *The Julianes* is an unfortunate exception in a noteworthy series including both *The Poor Little Carpenter* and *The Hermitage, the Fountain, and the River*, two plays that helped to assure Marquina's place in the history of contemporary Spanish theater.

CHAPTER 7

Religious Plays

I Introduction

THE third major category of Marquina's dramatic production — historical and rural plays are the other two — is his religious theater. This briefer series consists only of *El monje blanco (The White Monk)*, *Teresa de Jesús*, *María la viuda (María the Widow)*, premièred in 1930, 1932, and 1943 respectively, and the Theresian trilogy, *La alcaidesa de Pastrana (The Prioress of Pastrana)*, *Las cartas de la monja (The Nun's Letters)*, and *La muerte en Alba (Death at Alba)* staged during the years 1911–1913 and published under the joint title of *Pasos y trabajos de Santa Teresa de Jesús (Trials and Tribulations of Saint Teresa de Jesús)* in 1941. This category is essentially reduced to the first three titles, since *Teresa de Jesús* is a new, unified version of the same Theresian trilogy. Although few in numbers, *The White Monk*, *Teresa de Jesús*, and *María the Widow* are among Marquina's best plays, and only his rural dramas *The Poor Little Carpenter* and *The Hermitage, the Fountain, and the River* are comparable. Angel Valbuena Prat has stated that *The White Monk*, *Teresa de Jesús*, and *María the Widow* are Marquina's "three best works."[1] In his edition of *Teresa de Jesús* José Montero Alonso has described Marquina's religious dramas as follows: "*Teresa de Jesús* is in a trajectory that, although limited within Marquina's total theater, was cultivated passionately by him: plays of saintliness and religious fervor, of exaltation of the highest and purest virtues of the soul, of a human and philosophical lesson, in the manner of our miracle plays or of our philosophical-religious plays of the Classic theater."[2] Two of the plays are set in Spain, *Teresa de Jesús* and *María the Widow*, while *The White Monk* is located in an Italian village during the Middle Ages.

Marquina again uses his favorite device of opposing two women, but, as in his rural dramas, he has matured and uses the same elements with greater artistic skill. The plays are still designed for female protagonists, as evidenced by the titles. The third play is no exception since the white monk is a woman in disguise.

It is difficult to determine exactly why Marquina turned again to this type of theater after nearly two decades separating *The White Monk* from the Theresian trilogy produced during the years 1911–1913. *The White Monk* opened on February 5, 1930, precisely during the turbulent days after the fall of the dictator, General Miguel Primo de Rivera, January 28. The eight days between the two events is very likely a coincidence. However, it is entirely possible that Marquina's religious dramas were the playwright's response to the difficult sociopolitical situation in Spain during the period 1930–1943. Another possible reason is that Marquina who in 1930 had passed his fiftieth year, felt a personal need to write religious drama.

II   El monje blanco (The White Monk)

The play is subtitled "Pictures of a Primitive Legend." There are twelve "pictures" framed within three acts. As in Marquina's historical dramas, the plastic element is particularly important in *The White Monk*.[3] The locale is the Italian village of Belcaro and its Franciscan monastery during the Middle Ages. In Act I a friar has created a marvelous statue of the Virgin, which is the talk of the village. The Provincial Superior arrives to hear in confession a friar who has committed a crime. Via the simple-minded Fray Can the Superior learns that the friar in question is Fray Paracleto, the sculptor. Act II is devoted to Fray Paracleto's confession, interspersed, after brief blackouts, with flashbacks into his past. Paracleto is really Count Hugo del Saso who has had a son with Oriana, daughter of the bandit Capolupo. Urged on by his fiancée, the German princess Mina Amanda, Hugo has Oriana exiled and attempts to kill his infant son, Mayolín. He is stopped by Capolupo, who is killed in a fight between the two men, just as Fray Can appears. Torn by guilt, Hugo has spent five years as a hermit and then has entered the monastery where, unable to forget Oriana, he has created a statue of the Virgin in her image.

In Act III, the white monk, who is Oriana in disguise, succeeds in seeing Paracleto-Hugo, whom she still loves. Hugo's former haughtiness returns, and in anger he destroys the statue. Fray Can, to whom the Virgin has "appeared" on various occasions, believes that the statue *is* the Virgin and attempts to attack Hugo. The Provincial Superior arrives and states that in order to give Hugo eventual absolution, he will impose upon him the penitence of leaving the order. For one year he will serve Oriana and will create a new statue. Meanwhile Anabela, who has cared for Hugo and Oriana's son, ties him to a tree following Fray Can's advice that the child would soon have a mother. Oriana's discovery of Mayolín is witnessed by Fray Can and the villagers who think Oriana is the Virgin and that they are in the presence of a miracle. Marquina adds an epilogue in which after a year, Hugo is about to return to the convent. However, Oriana's love, which is forgiving, and that of Mayolín, convince him to stay. The Provincial Superior agrees with Hugo's choice and finally gives him absolution.

We have given the plot summary in greater detail due to the play's importance within Marquina's theater. However, our summary includes only some of its more salient aspects since the work is crammed with incidents and details. This is the play's principal fault and, initially, does not allow a clear-cut conflict raising and development.

Franciscan influence is, of course, obvious in the play's composition and is acknowledged by Marquina in a series of notes included in his complete works (*Works*, IV, 1349–50). The model for *The White Monk* is Spain's religious theater of the Golden Age. Angel Valbuena Prat has stated that "the work, perhaps only by coincidence, resembles a series of plays by Lope de Vega about rustic saints related to Fray Can" such as *El rústico del cielo (The Peasant from Heaven)* and *San Diego de Alcalá.*[4] The plot, however, has some aspects that recall the Romantic drama, *Don Alvaro o la fuerza del sino (Don Alvaro or the Force of Fate)* which are briefly as follows: (a) the protagonist who kills the father of the woman he loves; (b) his constant anguish over his crime throughout the play; (c) the mystery that hovers over his presence in the monastery, where as a penitent he attempts to forget. Of course, the playwright's viewpoints are diametrically opposed: pessimistic in the Romantic author and optimistic in Marquina.

The play's structure shows Marquina's improved dramatic craftsmanship. In it the author handles three levels: (1) the "reality" of the play that develops on stage just as any other work; (2) the retrospective scenes of Fray Paracleto's confession; (3) the "supernatural" level in which the Virgin, played by the same actress who plays Oriana, appears before Fray Can.

In *The White Monk* Marquina traces the sequence of crime, remorse, penitence, and redemption in the figure of Fray Paracleto-Hugo del Saso. The conflict is not clearly raised until the end of the second "picture" when Paracleto reveals his anguish to the Provincial Superior: "My soul/is a live coal and lives aflame./. . . Praying is not enough;/Suffering!;/neither is crying. . . . I would like a firebrand of faith/in which to burn myself and die/" (*Works*, IV, 727). The play's conflict centers around the frustrated attempt of Paracleto to expiate his crime. In his conception of Paracleto-Hugo, Marquina has created a complex character which he analyzes with skillful psychological penetration. The main flaw in Paracleto-Hugo's composition is the failure to provide transition "on stage" between the haughty and violent individual we observe at the end of the play and the humble family man who appears in the epilogue, after the passage of one year of "dramatic time."

The miracle of Hugo's change accomplished by Oriana is in keeping with Marquina's idealized concept of woman's role in the life of a man. Oriana continues his line of heroines who represent a source of tranquility and peace *vis-à-vis* life's vicissitudes. Rather than a lover, she is seen as a mother figure, following the pattern already evident in early plays, as with Escorpina in *Benvenuto Cellini*. This character's originality lies, however, in the dual role of Oriana-the Virgin which is dramatically quite effective.

Fray Can is exceptional in Marquina's theater; there is no other character like him. However, from the point of view of Franciscan literature he is a conventional figure. Marquina himself was aware of this character's conventional aspect, as shown when Fray Can is described by another friar: "In this house we have as in all monasteries/the uncouth friar. . . . The usual poor thing;/disgrace and ridicule of the order" (*Works*, IV, 721).

The White Monk is Marquina's most ambitious play. In it he makes use of more dramatic devices than in any other work. The author shows himself particularly adept at achieving an organic unity of the many parts and at maintaining dramatic coherence among the play's three levels. Angel Valbuena Prat has emphasized the importance of *The White Monk:* "The play . . . stands out within Spanish contemporary theater. It connects with the tradition of Lope and opens up the renewed possiblility of sacred drama theater, which in France has Claudel as its model. García Lorca himself, more advanced in the theater, and who in another way also ties in with Lope, lacks this religious base, without which Spanish tradition is truncated."[5]

III Teresa de Jesús

Whereas *The White Monk* is characterized by its complexity, Marquina's next religious play, *Teresa de Jesús*, is simple and direct. Valbuena Prat in his comparison of both plays has noted that "if *The White Monk* is the grand, dynamic and creative play, *Teresa* is the reflective and respectful work, full of unction and simpleness, characteristics necessary for the subject, seen from a human point of view."[6] There was risk inherent in putting on stage a historical character of the fame of Saint Teresa of Avila, especially since she is associated with expertise in the Castilian language. However, Marquina overcame both obstacles successfully. The play's outstanding feature is precisely the author's exceptional portrayal, both in action and speech, of the historical character.

The play is divided into six "Impressions." In the first of these, friends and partisans of the protagonist discuss the obstacles before Teresa in her effort to reform the Carmelite Order. Teresa's role is limited in this "print" to a brief appearance at the end when she convinces the bishop of Avila to receive the convent of San José that she hopes to found. The second "print" takes place in the Encarnación Convent where Teresa finds herself surrounded by enemies and intrigue. In spite of the threats of the prioress who opposes Teresa's plans, and of her particular enemy, the nun doña Beatriz de Espina, the future saint stands firm and leaves to start her own convent. "Impression" three is set in the new convent that Teresa has just founded. The hypocritical doña Beatriz arrives to advise Teresa to flee as the authorities are searching for her. Teresa refuses to escape and leaves with the constables firm in her faith in God. Ten years elapse between "impressions" three and four. The reform movement has prospered, and Teresa is in the province of Seville to found another convent. Most of this "impression" consists of a retrospective conversation between the discalced friars, Jerónimo

Gracián and Juan de la Cruz and the cleric Julián Dávila, in which
they discuss events of the past ten years. Doña Beatriz, ostensibly
changed, arrives and wishes to enter the new convent. Teresa,
whose role in the "impression" is again limited, accepts Beatriz
warily, not without warning Fray Jerónimo of the danger. In the
fifth "impression," true to her intriguing nature, Beatriz has falsely
declared that Fray Jerónimo is maintaining an illicit relation with
María de José, the convent's prioress. An already aged Teresa arrives and, in an act of humility before Beatriz, succeeds in obtaining
the nun's true repentance. It is in this scene that Teresa experiences
a mystic trance. The last "impression" takes place shortly before
Teresa's death. Exhausted by the years of effort, she is about to
leave for Alba de Tormes. Alone and terribly fatigued, Teresa, without saying goodbye to the nuns, leaves with Blas, the Castilian
peasant who has arrived to transport her.

Since his youth, Marquina had felt a particular attraction for Saint
Teresa of Avila, who also figured among his favorite authors. This
interest was shared by the famous Argentine actress, Lola Membrives, who asked Marquina in May of 1932 to redo his Theresian
trilogy of one-act plays: *La alcaidesa de Pastrana (The Prioress of
Pastrana), Las cartas de la monja (The Nun's Letters),* and *La
muerte en Alba (Death at Alba).* Marquina's changes consist essentially in selecting additional moments from Saint Teresa's life that
did not appear in the trilogy and in modifying the play's focus by
giving greater emphasis to the Theresian reform movement.
Another major change is the addition of the fictional character, doña
Beatriz.

The contents of the first play in the trilogy, *The Prioress of Pastrana,* presenting the political intrigues of the Princess of Eboli
during her stay in the convent of Pastrana, are not included in
Teresa de Jesús. The six "impressions" that form the structure of
Teresa de Jesús are closer thematically to the second play, *The Nun's
Letters,* which has as its historical basis the dispute between the
calced and discalced friars. The latter are represented in the play by
Fray Jerónimo Gracián and Fray Juan de la Cruz. Although the
future San Juan de la Cruz (Saint John of the Cross) is mentioned
often in this early play, he never appears. The title refers to Teresa's
letters, which secure help for Jerónimo and Juan de la Cruz. *Death
at Alba,* the work that closes the trilogy, would be a continuation of
the action that Marquina chose for the last "impression" in *Teresa de*

Jesús. In *Death at Alba* Marquina recreates the Saint's last hours of life in the convent at Alba de Tormes. She first appears old and sick in the one-act play, but still active in the reform movement. The play ends with Teresa's death, surrounded by the community of nuns.

For *Teresa de Jesús* Marquina selected moments from the last twenty years of the Saint's life. This period would cover from approximately the year 1562 when she founded her first convent to her death in Alba de Tormes in 1582. "The play does not really have a plot in the classic sense with the traditional formulas and channels: exposition, development, and resolution."[7] Each "impression" could be presented independently with the exception of the fourth one whose action is directly related to what occurs in the fifth. However, the connecting thread which gives unity to all six "impressions" is the figure of Teresa de Jesús and her reform movement. Marquina has stated that the figure of Teresa de Jesús "has for the stage amazing possibilities of variety and unity," which probably explains why in this play, more than in any other, he has stayed close to known historical facts.[8]

The Teresa de Jesús presented by Marquina is a Castilian woman with her feet firmly on the ground, in direct contact with the concrete reality of sixteenth-century Spain. According to Marquina, his intention was to "humanize" Teresa as much as possible.[9] This concept of the saint is synthesized in the following description contained in the first "impression": "If a Castilian nun/becomes a saint she shall do it/with the poise of a woman who does not deny being human" (*Works*, IV, 1184). Compared to the trilogy, in this play Marquina has given less emphasis to Teresa's mystic character. She experiences only one trance as opposed to two in *The Nun's Letters* and one in *Death at Alba*. Marquina's purpose was to present various facets of Teresa's personality. Thus we see her maternal with her nuns, dignified and sure of herself with the representatives of the law and her superiors, forceful and ironic with her enemies, capable of humbling herself before these very enemies if it is a question of saving a soul as with doña Beatriz, and proud of extolling divine love over earthly values. Marquina completes his characterization by capturing admirably in his verses the Saint's simple, unadorned language.

The play's ending is particularly effective, showing evident progress that differentiates the 1932 dramatist from the author who

wrote the trilogy during the years 1911–1913. In *Death at Alba* the
audience witnesses Teresa's death on stage as the play ends. In
Teresa de Jesús, Marquina leaves the ending "open" which greatly
increases the scene's dramatic impact. We see the Saint, old and
sick as she starts out on the road to Alba de Tormes with the peasant
Blas, symbol of Castile, on a trip that the audience perceives as
being her last.

In Beatriz the author has created a complex character in whose
soul struggle the forces of good and evil. According to Marquina,
Beatriz — the only important character who did not really exist —
is the figure "in which are personified the obstacles any reformer
will find in his way."[10] The future San Juan de la Cruz has a small
role limited almost exclusively to conversation with Fray Jerónimo
about Teresa and her work.

The request by Lola Membrives was the immediate stimulus that
convinced Marquina to redo his trilogy. Nevertheless the sociopolitical situation in Spain during the early 1930's might have also
sparked this new version. It was precisely in May of 1932 that the
burning of convents began in Madrid and shortly thereafter in the
provinces, including Valencia, Córdoba, Seville, Murcia, and especially Málaga. It is not difficult to conceive that *Teresa de Jesús* was
Marquina's answer to the offensive against the religious orders.
Whatever were the reasons behind the play, its première, according
to Isabel Snyder, acquired political significance: "Marquina wrote
his tribute to the beauty and strength of Teresa's character in his
play *Teresa de Jesús*, written in 1932 in the period when the leftists
were becoming openly hostile to anything typically Spanish or religious. On the night of the première, Marquina, upon taking leave
of his family, remarked: 'I do not know if I will end in jail this night,
but I have written what is in my heart about the saint.' Despite the
antagonistic air gathering in Spain at that time against religion, the
play was a huge success."[11] The following year, José María Pemán,
possibly influenced by Marquina, premièred a play, *El divino im-
paciente (The Impatient Saint)* based on the life of Saint Francis
Xavier. The work clearly had political aims and was its author's
response to the same turbulent events.

The figure of Saint Teresa has attracted many Spanish dramatists,
among them Lope de Vega who first put the Saint of Avila in a play.
Juan Emilio Aragonés has stated that "after many appearances of
Saint Teresa as a figure of our theater — all of them in the seven-

teenth century —, it is necessary to jump to the present to find another worthy contribution: Marquina's. . . ."[12] It is interesting to note that among Marquina's prolific dramatic production, *Teresa de Jesús* is his favorite play (*Works*, IV, 1352).

IV   María la viuda (María the Widow)

During the 1930's and early 1940's, Marquina's dramatic output decreased considerably. These were the years of the Civil War and difficult postwar period. Those plays he did write are rather run-of-the-mill, far below the artistic level achieved in *Teresa de Jesús*.[13] However, in 1943, just three years before his death, Marquina created perhaps his best drama, *María the Widow*. In his biography of the dramatist, José Montero Alonso has described reaction to the play's initial staging: "The dramatic poem is a great success: the greatest success achieved by Marquina after the war and one of the warmest and most profitable of his theatrical life. Praise, official recognition — the cross of Alfonso the Wise — the play's run extending for days . . . on the Lara stage with constant warm and popular applause."[14]

María the Widow is divided into two acts, each of which contains four scenes. During the first six scenes Marquina develops two parallel actions which finally blend together in scenes five and six. The first scene is devoted to Paula, a woman who in her youth wanted to be a nun but had been obliged by her parents to marry. She explains to her brother, the hermit Simplicio, that with her husband dead and her daughter Isidora about to marry Dionisio, she can finally enter a convent. Marquina initiates the second action in scene 2 in which we meet the widowed village butcher, María, and her son Nacín, a young donjuanesque type. This scene revolves around a dagger that María refuses to sell to the mayor, Pero, as it once belonged to her husband. As the scene ends, Nacín, aware of its hiding place, surreptitiously takes the dagger. Scene 3 shifts to a secret meeting between Nacín and Isidora before a mill. They have fallen in love while scarcely knowing each other. Nacín enters the mill to investigate a noise. In an ensuing struggle off-stage, Dionisio kills Nacín with the latter's own dagger. The next scene takes place the following day. In spite of the fact that Isidora will be left alone — Dionisio has fled — Paula refuses to stay with her and

enters the convent. The action then returns to María, who, unaware
of her son's death, has been waiting three years for his return. Gil
Molino, a young bandit pursued by the law, is given refuge by María
whose maternal instincts are aroused by the newcomer's resemblance to her son. In scene 6, Paula after only two years in the
convent has become prioress and has acquired the reputation of a
saint. Alone before a crucifix, she asks if there is another soul who
can surpass the perfection she has reached. Her recently deceased
brother Simplicio appears before her and declares that there are
many, but there is one above all. She lives in a village and Paula will
recognize her by her bloodied arms. The prioress decides to search
out this woman.

Scene 7 takes place in the village market where Paula comes upon
María with her arms bloodied by the meat she has been butchering.
The prioress, however, is doubtful and only asks María directions to
the church. Pero, the mayor, who suspects María is hiding the
bandit, displays the dagger and convinces her that Gil Molino is her
son's murderer. In the last scene, after an inner struggle, María
overcomes her doubts and continues to hide Gil Molino who is
really Dionisio. Paula, who arrives at María's house by chance,
discovers that there is a man in hiding and suspects that it is the
widow's lover. María, who has had enough of Paula's accusations,
reveals that the man is her son's murderer. This confession convinces Paula she has found the woman mentioned by Simplicio.
María surrenders to the mayor, but Dionisio, who has not fled, gives
himself up instead. As the play ends María remains free, and Paula
vows to use her influence as prioress to help Dionisio.

The play's structure is closer to the complexity of *The White
Monk* than the simple lines of *Teresa de Jesús*. The two parallel
actions do not follow the same chronological order, as shown by
scenes 5 and 6. Scene 5, which deals with María, takes place three
years after the murder, whereas in the following scene, with Paula
already a prioress, only two years have elapsed. At times, some
secondary characters appear in both actions, but in reality both
María and Paula develop independently of each other during the
first six scenes. However, at the same time, in spite of their independence, both actions complement each other, creating a sort of
contrapuntal effect.

The source of *María the Widow* is found in the same popular
legend used by Tirso de Molina for his play, *El condenado por*

desconfiado (The Condemned Doubter). Marquina had read this legend in Ramón Menéndez Pidal's *Estudios literarios (Literary Studies)*.[15] As in the case of *The Condemned Doubter*, the nucleus of *María the Widow* is the confrontation between two principal characters: Paulo and Enrico in Tirso's play and Paula — note the similarity of names — and María in Marquina's work. In both plays, the main characters are symbolic representations of different theological viewpoints. Paulo and Enrico represent the doctrine of predestination and free will respectively. The focus of *María the Widow* is described by Marquina as follows: "The action revolves around the central problem of our Catholic doctrine: salvation through faith alone, in a rapture of absolute perfection transporting us . . . from this world, or salvation through faith and good works, promoting the good of others, suffering with them, forgiving them their insults and offenses. Naturally I am inclined toward our Spanish way of feeling religion and faith. . . . That is, to save our souls by doing good for others, for the love of God."[16]

The idea of doing good for others is a doctrine that, expressed or implied, Marquina often extols in his theater. In *María the Widow*, the author was not interested primarily in presenting and defending a theological doctrine as was Tirso de Molina. The intellectual aspect of the contending points of view could represent only a limited attraction for the theatergoing public in 1943. More interesting would be Paula and María's human conflict and the Christian spirit embodied in the play that allows a mother to forgive the murderer of her only son. It must be kept in mind that Spain in 1943 was suffering the after-effects of her civil war. Only four years separate the première of *María the Widow* and the bloody struggle in which brother fought against brother. The audience more than likely captured the play's underlying relation with the events in Spain during the late 1930's and early 1940's. The critic Nicolás González Ruiz who holds a somewhat similar view of the play's reconciling intent has attributed to *María the Widow* a focus beyond events in Spain when he states that in the conflict of Paula and María are brought to life the problems that distort the world's peace at the time Marquina is writing. . . . The greatness of María the widow who sees her son in the enemy, is Marquina's major concern."[17]

María the widow represents the maximum development of the idealized woman in the author's dramatic production. Pilar Díez-Jiménez Castellanos has noted that "the theater and all the works of

Marquina are a shrine raised in honor of a woman, although she is
not a complete and real woman, since the poet is not so objective,
but rather the ideal of a woman that his artist's imagination has
fashioned."[18] As we have noted in our analysis of *The White Monk*,
Marquina tends to see woman in a man's life more as a mother figure
than as a lover. In *María the Widow* Marquina totally eliminates the
amorous aspect and presents only the essence of the woman as
mother.

Marquina has been able to avoid having his characters reduced to
mere abstractions of their symbolic roles. Paula and above all,
María, are exceptionally well drawn. María the widow is perhaps
Marquina's most outstanding character. In contrast to María, the
incarnation of Christian kindness and sacrifice, the author offers
Paula's egocentrism. The latter, in spite of her daughter's need for
help, has only one thought, to enter the convent and achieve
spiritual perfection: "And I want perfection:/I don't know how to
turn back!" (*Works*, V, 768). Marquina, however, has been careful
not to trace only one aspect of Paula's personality. Through her
haughtiness there is still visible the maternal feeling that the
dramatist looks for in a woman. María's crisis occurs when she discovers that Gil Molino is her son's murderer. She not only overcomes her doubts as to her feelings, but is also able to say "Goodbye, son," as the law takes Dionisio away. A villager indignant over
María's farewell asks how far must forgiveness go. The play's Christian spirit is summed up when María answers that it will continue
"until goodness, which is a soft yoke/triumphs over old hatreds,/ . . .
until accomplishing what Christ said/on the cross before dying!/until
the son resuscitates in the murderer"(*Works*, V, 899).

Although the joint protagonists dominate the action, *María the
Widow* is one of the plays in which Marquina has expended most
care in his characterization of the secondary roles. The mayor, Pero,
is an admirable synthesis of humaneness and justice. Various aspects
of his personality are reminiscent of Pedro Crespo, the protagonist
of Calderón de la Barca's *El alcalde de Zalamea* (*The Mayor of
Zalamea*). Simpicio's direct, "simple" faith serves as a contrast to his
sister's egocentric spiritual yearnings. Isidora in her role of abandoned daughter recalls the orphaned Susina in Marquina's *The Poor
Little Carpenter*. However, the two youths, though well characterized through their contrasting personalities, do not reach the
artistic level of Pero and Simpicio.

María the Widow is easily the play in which Marquina has been most successful in achieving an organic fusion of the dramatic components. Valbuena Prat has stated in reference to this play that "the characters, the two protagonists as well as the secondary figures, are drawn with unsurpassable vigor; the plot, varied in its scenes and essential in its foundations, develops with knowing ability; and its resolution, in keeping with the development, crowns this work: as a whole the poet's most perfect drama."[19]

CHAPTER 8

Contemporary Plays

I Introduction

M ARQUINA'S contemporary plays are the least-known group-
ing of his dramatic works. They have remained buried within
his copious theatrical production, eclipsed by the historical plays
with which the author is generally identified. We include in this
category of contemporary plays those works written in prose —
along with two exceptions in verse — with an urban setting and
which take place during a period contemporary to their writing.
Two of the plays are set in the country, but the main characters are
generally from the city and the rural environment does not significantly influence the works. The protagonists are still female, and
although love is the most prevalent theme, the plays, particularly
those written circa 1918–1919, do offer some variety. However,
Marquina's best contemporary plays are those in which the author
studies the feminine psyche with love as a background.

The span of the dramatist's contemporary plays extends from
Cuando florezcan los rosales (When the Roses Bloom) to *Lo que Dios
no perdona (What God Does Not Forgive)*, premièred in 1913 and
1935 respectively.[1] Within this category there are three distinguish-
able periods: (1) The contemporary plays Marquina would occasionally write while still concentrating on his historical theater. These
plays and the year they were staged are: *Cuando florezcan los
rosales (When the Roses Bloom)*, 1913; *La hiedra (Ivy)*, 1914; and
Una mujer (One Woman), 1915. (2) The four plays the author wrote
after he abandoned verse to "escape" from the "affectation" of his
poetic theater. These are *Alondra (Skylark)*, *Dondiego de Noche
(Mr. Night Flower)*, *Alimaña (Vixen)*, and *La extraña (The
Stranger)*, all written in 1918 and 1919. (3) His last works of this
type, spread over the period 1928–1935, including *La reina del*

92

mundo (Queen of the World), *Sin horca ni cuchillo (Without a Weapon)*, and *Lo que Dios no perdona (What God Does Not Forgive)*, and *La vida es más (There's More to Life)*.

An analysis of Marquina's contemporary plays reveals that this type of theater was ill suited to his particular dramatic talents. It is obvious that he was functioning outside of his *forte*, dramatic verse, in a setting far removed in time and place from that of the audience. Marquina's contemporary plays never seem to fully develop and lack the spark characteristic of his better verse dramas. The author's willingness to write this type of theater can be explained by his expressed desire to expand the limits of his theatrical production (*Works*, III, 1352). On the other hand these plays also reveal Marquina's attempt to adapt his theater — at least in part — to the theater-going audience's taste, epitomized by Jacinto Benavente and his followers during the first third of the twentieth century.

II   Cuando florezcan los rosales (When the Roses Bloom)

In *When the Roses Bloom*, Marquina deals with one of his favorite subjects, a woman's reaction to the long, difficult process of reaching true love. The play, set in the country among summer residents from Madrid, revolves around Agueda, a young doctor who believes she is in love with the playboy, Jorge Valtierra. The latter is also loved by Lolín, a frail, sickly young lady who is a patient of Agueda's father. The play's conflict springs from the struggle between Agueda's feelings for Jorge and the great affection she feels for Lolín. Marquina traces the transformation of Agueda's sentiments up to the ultimate realization that she does not love Jorge, but rather her father's friend, the reliable and good-hearted Salazar.

In *When the Roses Bloom* Marquina, more completely than in any previous play, defines the concept of love which he will propagate during the entirety of his dramatic career. For Marquina, the path to true love is long and painful. Only through suffering can one reach true love, and as Salazar states, "life is morally incomplete without love" (*Works*, II, 154). Marquina's theater abounds in female protagonists who must overcome a series of difficult obstacles before achieving true love. The play's title refers to one of the author's favorite metaphors. The flowering rose, which represents the culmination of love, frequently appears in both his theater and poetry, although never invested with as much importance as in *When the Roses Bloom*.

III   La Hiedra (Ivy) *and* Una mujer (One Woman)

In 1914, while still immersed in his production of historical verse plays Marquina turned again briefly to prose and wrote *Ivy*, a melodramatic work set in the "present." Carmen, obsessed with the idea of rising above what she considers the sordid environment in which she lives, has an affair with a government official she thinks will further her husband's career. Discovered by her father, Carmen confesses the truth to her husband Pablo. The play ends as Carmen's father, who is mentally unbalanced, takes an ax and kills her.

Marquina's attitude towards Carmen's transgression reflects the "traditional" perspective of Spanish dramaturgy: bloody vengeance by the cuckolded husband (although in this case the father is the executioner). In *Alimaña (Vixen)* premièred in 1919 and in one of his early plays, *Mala cabeza (Ne'er-do-well)*, Marquina adopts a more modern attitude and limits the effects of a wife's adultery to the couple's separation. However, in another play, *La vida es más (There's More to Life)*, Marquina pardons a husband's infidelity.

Una mujer (One Woman), the last of the contemporary plays Marquina wrote during the height of his historical theater, is one of his weaker efforts. The plot concerns Pilar, who for ten years has been both teacher and substitute mother for Carmina, only daughter of the rakish widowed Lorenzo. This don Juan finally realizes that he will find true love with Pilar, that is, with one woman.

IV   *The Departure from Verse*

During the years 1918–1919 Marquina markedly increased his production of contemporary plays. In the notes included in his complete works the author states that during the period 1916–1920 he attempted to escape from the "affectation" of his historical theater by temporarily abandoning verse and writing a series of prose plays: "I shall cite, without hesitation, *Dondiego de Noche (Mr. Night Flower)* with my good-bye to a Madrid that no longer exists and which at the time we were ready to bury; *La princesa juega (The Princess Amuses Herself)* with the first inklings and the initial description of the realistic politician about to make his appearance; and *La extraña (The Stranger)* where a ghostlike Russia, still in its literary or, if you will, novelistic aspect, but already with a manifest allusion to possible derivations, was making its presence felt in the Spanish consciousness" *(Works,* III, 1352).[2]

In the notes Marquina does not mention *Alondra (Skylark),* another contemporary prose play written during this period. Although the play was staged on April 5, 1918, apparently it was never published. Don Luis Marquina, the dramatist's son has indicated that the play was not included in his father's complete works "because a major part of the file and library of Eduardo Marquina was ransacked during the years 1936–1939 when his house was occupied by red militia-men."[3]

In 1918, besides *Skylark,* Marquina wrote *Mr. Night Flower,* a play that was staged the following year.[4] The Madrid that "no longer exists" referred to by Marquina in the previously quoted notes is that of 1900. The play's action, which recalls Benavente's turn-of-the-century plays of social criticism such as *Gente conocida (Well-known People),* develops between two levels of society: one rich and the other poor. Juanito Carmona, whose family has seen better days, moves in both worlds. The play's conflict is raised by the clash within Juanito between these two worlds.

Marquina gives the play an interesting social content as he censures the hypocritical, false, and empty life of Madrid high society. However, he also criticizes the social structure of the times divided between two extremes: rich and poor. When Juanito is asked why he did not go to his friends when his family was in need, he replies: "To enter and leave, all doors are open. To stay, none. In a country like ours, in this Madrid, where there are only two extremes, head and tail, aristocracy and the lower classes, separated from one, you are rejected by the other" *(Works,* III, 71). This aspect of *Mr. Night Flower* is rather unique in Marquina's theater, which loses its social concerns after 1908, the year that marks the end of the author's youthful nonconformist attitude.

Alimaña (Vixen), written in 1919, deals with, according to Marquina, "the subject of the falling apart of the Christian family" *(Works,* III, 1352).[5] The author, however, has difficulties in developing this theme as the work resembles more a conventional story of adultery. Set in the Pyrenees, although all the principal characters are from the city, the plot deals with the affair the writer, Román, is having with Valentina (who is married to Alberto). This triangle is complicated by Laura, Alberto's younger sister, who falls in love with Román. As we have noted, in *Vixen* Marquina adopts a more liberal attitude toward a wife's infidelity — the couple separates — than in *Ivy* where the same transgression is punished by death.

Marquina also had difficulties with the ideological background of his contemporary play, *La extraña (The Stranger)*, a work that apparently was never staged. Two mysterious Russians, Gavrilo and Sonia, who falsely claim to be brother and sister, arrive at an inn. Pedro, son of the inn's owners falls in love with Sonia. The latter, however, feels that her "dark" past is an obstacle to happiness with Pedro, takes poison, and dies.

If we follow Marquina's previously quoted statement that in *The Stranger*, "a ghostlike Russia . . . was making its presence felt in the Spanish consciousness," and match it to the plot, it seems that the author intended to express the significance of the Bolshevist revolution — symbolized by the nefarious Gavrilo — that had triumphed in 1917, just two years before the play's writing. However, in *The Stranger*, Marquina — too far afield from his usual thematic material — was unable to develop clearly the play's ideology.

The lack of success with these contemporary plays written in the period 1916–1919 apparently convinced Marquina that they were not the proper direction for expanding the limits of his theater. In 1920 he stopped writing contemporary prose plays and turned once again to verse for his historical drama *Ebora*.

V *Last Contemporary Plays*

Marquina did not return to contemporary plays until 1928, when he wrote *La reina del mundo (Queen of the World)*. In this work, Marquina who usually tended to construct his plays well within established theatrical canons, experiments with technique and borrows elements from the cinema. The play is subtitled "Symphony on Cinema Motifs" and requires for its development seven settings, each of which is enclosed within a framework of curtains that "will not necessarily have to be changed" (*Works*, IV, 159). One result of this structure, however, is an extremely long play, burdened by too many situations and events.

In his characterization of the protagonist, Marquina is on more familiar ground as he studies the feminine psychology of Albertina Davidson whose conflict stems from her effort to achieve self-fulfillment. Albertina, who was played by the famous actress, Margarita Xirgu, is a cold, calculating woman who thinks only of herself. She rejects the love offered by Max in order to affirm her own personality freely and live her own life. Her efforts, however, lead to unhappiness, and she unsuccessfully attempts suicide. Finally, after many years, she realizes the error of her ways and decides that life is still worth living if you live to help others.

In comparison with the "new" liberated woman offered by Ibsen in *A Doll's House,* Marquina views a woman's happiness as being achieved through sacrifice for the good of others. At times, interwoven within this concept, the author alludes tenuously to maternity as one path toward happiness. It is interesting to note that the author has not given the play a Spanish setting. There are some references that seem to point to the U.S.A., but generally the play has an international air that recalls somewhat Benavente's *La noche del sábado (The Witches' Sabbath).*

Within the same year, 1928, Marquina wrote the first of his two contemporary verse plays, *La vida es más (There's More to Life).* The playwright, however, had difficulty in adapting his dramatic verse to a contemporary urban setting. Enrique de Mesa has described *There's More to Life* as "a confused play, cold, slow and arbitrary."[6] Nevertheless, the work does help to further define Marquina's traditional concept of women, as observed in *Queen of the World.*

Don Fernando Olivar is an aging Don Juan who eventually discovers that there is more to life than his romantic escapades and returns, not without reluctance, to his family and is welcomed gladly. Adelaida, Fernando's wife has nothing in common with Nora, Ibsen's heroine in *A Doll's House.* Through Adelaida, Marquina reaffirms the traditional role of the Spanish mother, capable of great sacrifice — even to accepting her husband's infidelity — in order to maintain the well-being of her family unit. Marquina shares this traditional attitude with other contemporary dramatists. Although the following statement is made in reference to Marquina's *When the Roses Bloom,* it is more *à propos* to *There's More to Life:*

"Marquina like Benavente and Martínez Sierra answers the moral
question raised by Ibsen in *A Doll's House* in terms of a mother's
duty to her children."[7]

The following year, 1929, Marquina wrote another contemporary
play in verse, *Sin horca ni cuchillo (Without a Weapon)*. The play's
locale is a village where a group from Madrid has arrived to make a
movie, set in the sixteenth century. Gonzalo de Torre, who is a
descendent of the region's lords, has the main role. He courts and
promises to marry a local girl, Galiana, who is also in the film along
with other villagers. Gonzalo, however, reneges on his promise, and
Galiana, crushed, incites her jealous boyfriend, Sotero, to kill her.

A notable feature of the work's structure is Marquina's able utili-
zation of the "play within a play" technique in the first act in which
he fuses the play's "reality" with that of the film. The playwright,
however, did not fully exploit the possibilities of this technique, and
after Act I, *Without a Weapon* develops along the structural lines of
his previous contemporary plays.

In *Without a Weapon*, as in *There's More to Life,* Marquina has
not been able to successfully adapt his dramatic verse to contemporary dialogue. This difficulty calls attention to a characteristic problem of verse theater in the twentieth century. Theater audiences
have grown accustomed to prose as the dramatist's medium of expression. In plays with a present day-realistic setting, there is resis-
tance on the part of the audience to hearing their contemporaries
speaking in verse. The same audience, however, will more readily
accept a verse play if the setting is far away in time and space, as in
the case of a historical drama.

Marquina apparently realized or intuited the difficulties inherent
in writing a contemporary play in verse; the only time he used prose
again was to write precisely this type of drama, a work entitled *Lo
que Dios no perdona (What God Does Not Forgive)*. In a review of
the play published in the *Heraldo de Madrid*, March 23, 1935,
Antonio de Obregón quoted Marquina as stating that he had
selected prose for *What God Does Not Forgive* in order to "express
himself freely, to picture an event of our world and of our times that
fits badly within poetic forms. He has tried to offer us characters in
daily dress and events that take place in today's drawing rooms and
has been tempted by the freedom offered by prose and everyday
dialogues. . . ."

What God Does Not Forgive suffered a fate similar to another contemporary play, *Skylark*, in that it was not included in Marquina's complete works since the manuscript was lost along with a major part of the author's library during the Spanish Civil War. Marquina's family has been able to conserve only an incomplete manuscript. The plot, familiar in Marquina's theater, involves two women, Dina and Ventura, who compete for the love of Enrique who is married to Ventura but loves Dina. Lacking a complete manuscript we cannot, of course, evaluate the play. Antonio Obregón's review extolled the work's virtues, while Enrique Díez-Canedo in *La Voz*, also on March 23, 1935, was more reserved in his praise.

What God Does Not Forgive is the last of Marquina's contemporary plays. Although the author, in his efforts to widen the scope of his theater, added new themes, such as those of *Vixen* and *The Stranger*, and attempted different theatrical techniques in *Queen of the World* and *Without a Weapon*, he was clearly cultivating a genre unsuited to his talents which lay in verse plays separated in time and place from the audience.

CHAPTER 9

Miscellaneous Plays

I Introduction

MARQUINA'S dramatic production offers considerably more variety than that historical theater inspired in Spain's past with which he is usually identified. Many of his plays do not fall within the categories utilized in previous chapters. This variety is due largely to Marquina's reiterated desire to expand the limits of his theater.[1] Another reason, obviously related to the first, is that Marquina lived on what his writings produced. The author never reached a level of economic security that would have allowed him to stop composing plays. In 1946, a few days before his death in New York, Marquina stated the following: "You know that although I am a bit more than sixty years old — let us not talk about the bit — I have to work constantly, because I live almost from day to day. It is true that with my plays I earned some two million pesetas. But I can hardly count on anything more than what I collect in a year: today some 80,000 pesetas."[2]

Marquina knew that to make his living from the theater he had to vary his dramatic production and to create plays acceptable to the theater audiences that had followed his premières since his first success in 1908 with *The Daughters of the Cid,* the play that marks his definite break with his youthful rebellious spirit. Thus, although Marquina varied his theatrical production, his plays were generally constructed within established dramatic canons familiar to his audiences.

Of the ten plays included in this chapter, easily the most outstanding is *Don Luis Mejía,* written in collaboration with the Cuban diplomat and author, Alfonso Hernández Catá. Special attention will be given to this drama, and our analysis of the remaining dramas will concentrate on their most significant aspects.

100

II   *Three Troubadour Plays*

During the years 1910–1912 Marquina wrote three verse plays with troubadour settings: *El rostro ideal (A Certain Face), El último día (The Last Day),* and *El rey trovador (The Troubadour King).* The first of these, *A Certain Face,* written in 1910 and never staged, is of particular interest because Marquina wanted the Guerrero-Mendoza company to put on this work and not *The Sun Has Set in Flanders,* which eventually became his most famous work. *A Certain Face* is clearly inferior to *The Sun Has Set in Flanders.* The troubadour play is extremely long, full of incidents and digressions, and suffers from an overpopulation of characters. In *A Certain Face* Marquina extols the power of love to convert the adventurous, warlike princess Dora, before whom all men succumb, into a woman in love after meeting Ladislao, King of Poland. As in most of Marquina's plays written during this period, an overabundance of lyricism reduces the work's dramatic content. Marquina himself recognized the play's defects: "The troubadour world that I set myself to evoke and that I had studied at that time had not yet taken root in my soul. . . . I apparently was not entirely satisfied with the result, since on two occasions whatever it is in the play that had not been expressed struggled to come to the surface in other works. First in that jail ballad, *The Last Day.* . . . And finally in *The Troubadour King* . . . where the troubadour world that had had time to crystallize within me was able to surface naturally during the composition and reach the point of expressive maturity that it required" (*Works,* I, 1238).

Less pretentious and simpler than *A Certain Face,* but also suffering from excessive lyricism, *The Last Day* is a brief one-act play with a prologue, dedication, and epilogue. Its action is limited to a farewell meeting between Prince Reno and Dina, the jailer's daughter, who deeply love each other. The prince's forces have triumphed and he will be king after an imprisonment of ten years. The struggle between duty and love is settled and Reno bids Dina farewell forever.

The last play in this series, *The Troubadour King* is by far the most dramatically effective. The progress Marquina referred to above is manifest. The play's structure is firmer than a *A Certain Face,* and the dramatist's hand is surer as he handles the work's different component parts. Nevertheless, as in the two previous works, in *The Troubadour King* excessive lyricism obstructs the dramatic development. The most outstanding feature in *The Troubadour King* is the dramatically effective tragic sadness that envelops the lover's triangle formed by Queen Laura de Lil of Provence and the two brothers Guillermo and Arnaldo de Faidit. The love that both brothers hold for this sort of *femme fatale* drives them toward death: Guillermo loses his life on the battlefield and Arnaldo commits suicide.

Pilar Díez-Jiménez Castellanos has explained as follows the presence of the troubadour theme in Marquina's theater: "It is logical that the troubadours attracted Marquina. He was driven by all that was indefinite and poetic."[3] The troubadour theme lent itself to the lyrical quality which characterized the literature of the times. Two of the Hispanic world's most noted literary figures, Ruben Darío and Ramón del Valle-Inclán, were attracted by the troubadour world. The latter used the troubadours as source materials in his play *Cuento de abril (April Tale)*, premièred on May 19, 1910, a date that coincides approximately with the writing of *A Certain Face*.[4]

III   *A Play for Children*

Around 1910, Marquina wrote a short play for children in six scenes entitled *La muñeca irrompible (The Unbreakable Doll)*.[5] Although the play as a whole has no great significance within the development of Marquina's theater, the stage technique utilized is worth noting. As Baby, accompanied by her brother, is playing with her dolls, a violet light floods the stage. The children find that the dolls have disappeared and have been replaced by huge dolls exactly the same as the originals. The dolls come to life and the children discover that they are in the kingdom of the evil Protocolo. After a frightening adventure they are saved by one of the dolls, Polichinela. They then wake up and discover that it was only a dream.

The above schematic plot summary is sufficient to illustrate how Marquina, albeit on a simple level, was creating a "play within a play."[6] In this respect the author anticipates a similar but more complex structure utilized on a higher intellectual level by Jacinto Grau in *El señor de Pigmalión (Mr. Pygmalion)*, published in Madrid in 1921 and premièred in Paris in 1925. There is no implication in the above statement of any direct influence. Behind these plays we have the legend of Pygmalion and Galatea and, of course, the theatrical tradition of a "play within a play" that includes in Spanish literature works by Cervantes, Calderón, Manuel Tamyo y Baus, and Marquina's contemporary, Manuel Linares Rivas in *Almas brujas* (Wicked Souls). In other literatures the obvious example is Shakespeare's *Hamlet,* Pirandello's *Sei personaggi in cerca d'autore (Six Characters in Search of an Author),* and the Czech Karel Capek's *R.U.R..* Although Marquina's effort is a very modest one, his name should be added to the long list of dramatists who have used this technique in the twentieth century.

IV   La princesa juega (The Princess Amuses Herself)

The Princess Amuses Herself, staged in 1920, is another drama written during the years 1916–1920 when, in order to escape from the "affectation" of the historical verse theater then in vogue, Marquina abandoned verse and wrote a series of prose plays. All except *The Princess Amuses Herself* have a contemporary setting. Marquina states that *The Princess Amuses Herself* contains "the first inklings and the initial description of the realistic politician about to make his appearance" (*Works,*III,1352). While this concept is evident in the play, it appears in diluted form. *The Princess Amuses Herself* is one more effort to trace the difficult path a woman must tread in order to achieve true love.

The protagonist, Princess Casilda, is bored and to support her whims war is declared. She eventually falls in love with her political enemy, the minister Hilario, and it is love that changes for the better this vain and egotistical woman. The rest of the plot seems borrowed with slight variations from Marquina's troubadour play, *The Last Day.* Hilario and Princess Casilda cannot marry because of their different status. Hilario is a jailer's son. The play ends as the couple separate forever. *The Princess Amuses Herself* never really shows signs of life and is one of the dramatist's less successful efforts.

V   *Two "Oriental" Plays*

Marquina wrote two plays with an oriental setting, *El pavo real (The Peacock)* and *Era una vez en Bagdad (Once Upon a Time in Baghdad,* staged in 1922 and 1932 respectively. It is interesting to note that this type of exotic setting (in the literature of the times identified with "Modernism"), appears relatively late in Marquina's theater. In the notes included with *Once Upon a Time in Baghdad* he explains how he originally came to select an oriental setting: "Gregorio Martínez Sierra, at the time director of the Eslava Theater, gave me the complete subject of *The Peacock*. He had seen it in an English narrative" (*Works,*IV,1351). This statement would have to be related to a comment made by Pilar Díez-Jiménez Castellanos who stated that the première of *The Peacock* was met by certain accusations of plagiarism of Oscar Wilde, but that Marquina's name was saved by blaming his collaborator.[7] We have not encountered any additional references to this situation. Apparently it was of minor importance and soon forgotten.

In spite of *The Peacock*'s "ornamentation" and exotic oriental background, the plot is simple, direct, and without digressions. In *The Peacock*, as in *Once Upon a Time in Baghdad*, the poet Marquina dominates the dramatist. Prince Deli before becoming king goes out into the world to gain experience. He falls in love with a poor girl, Aissa, and they have two children. At the end of two blissful years, Deli must return to the palace. After seven years a vizier arrives and takes away the children. Heartbroken, Aissa asks a wizard to change her into a peacock so that she can visit her children in the palace. Finally, Prince Deli, who had been suffering from amnesia, regains his memory and the entire family is joyfully reunited.

Aissa is a *tour de force* role for the feminine protagonist that generally dominates Marquina's plays. The prince's role is limited to the first part of the play and another brief appearance at the end. Aissa is a typical Marquina heroine: an idealized woman who is the embodiment of sacrifice and self-denial. To achieve true love she must overcome a series of painful obstacles. In spite of her basically lyrical character, Aissa, who was played by the famous actress Catalina Bárcena, is well drawn.

Marquina's second oriental play, *Once Upon a Time in Baghdad*, is more complex and ambitious than *The Peacock*. Marquina has stated that after writing the latter work he took a liking to "the exceptional charm of oriental literature" and that he continued reading *A Thousand and One Nights*, jotting down ideas for future plays (*Works,*IV,1351). Harum, a poor man who appears in some of the stories, was the figure that most attracted Marquina, who decided to make him the protagonist of *Once Upon a Time in Baghdad*. The plot is extremely long and burdened by events and digressions.

Harum is a poor fisherman to whom material things are not important. He would like to buy Saleya for a wife, but since he lacks
money, her father sells her to Abu-Ishak. Harum ends up falling in
love with Sulima, favorite of the emperor Soleimán. The latter
realizes that Sulima loves Harum and frees her. The marriage of
Sulima based on love is a happy one, while Saleya and Abu-Ishak,
who have a material attitude toward life, live in constant conflict.

Within Marquina's theater characterized by feminine figures in
the main roles, *Once Upon a Time in Baghdad* offers special interest
since it is the only time a masculine protagonist totally dominates a
play. All the characters pale beside Harum. Harum represents
Marquina's concept of pure love, free from material considerations.
However, he is not simply a one-dimensional character. In addition
to being good and generous, he is also "impetuous, flowing over
with life, given to the voluptuousness of the moment, primitive,
coarse, and childish."[8]

In *Once Upon a Time in Baghdad* Marquina has made a special
appeal to the audience's visual and aural sensibility. His verses
recall the lyrical outbursts of earlier plays and include one of those
descriptive "arias" in which the author interrupts the play's dramatic development to "sing" of some particular object, person, or place
(in this case, the city of Baghdad) (*Works*, IV, 1050–51). The play's
plastic intent is indicated by its subtitle: "Impressions from A
Thousand and One Nights." To this end Marquina utilizes a cast of
twenty-four, frequent scenery changes, the accumulation of color-
fully dressed characters on stage, and the reproduction of pictur-
esque places such as the palace and harem. The play's construction,
however, is rather loose, and Marquina has not been able to achieve
a fusion of its component parts. Interestingly enough the dramatist
has indicated a particular liking for the play: "Although this doesn't
mean anything to its credit, *Once Upon a Time in Baghdad* is one of
the plays I prefer and that has pleased me particularly among my
works" (*Works*, IV, 1351–52). *Once Upon a Time in Baghdad*, however, did not attain the success enjoyed by *The Peacock*, which was
considerable.

VI El camino de la felicidad (The Road to Happiness)

In 1924 Marquina wrote in collaboration with Gregorio Martínez
Sierra *The Road to Happiness*, a work in which the authors unsuc-

cessfully attempted to create a poetic climate around the trials and
tribulations of the orphaned Blanca Rosa. In different stages she
leaves her step-mother, serves as a guide to a blind old man, works
for a farm couple, and lives with gypsies. She finally meets an aviator who saves her from death and both apparently live happily ever
after. Although the above structure might recall to some the
picaresque novel, Blanca Rosa has really none of the characteristics
generally attributed to protagonists of that genre.

   The Road to Happiness is a poor mixture of widely disparate
elements that range from a melodramatic fight between two gypsies
to the ethereal scenes that envelop Blanca Rosa's meeting with the
aviator. "The subject," states Díez-Canedo, "in itself is like any
other. It is presented with little originality, constructed scene by
scene, with a certain affected naïveté. . . ."[9]

VII   Don Luis Mejía

   Don Luis Mejía, written in 1925 in collaboration with the Cuban
author and diplomat, Alfonso Hernández Catá, is the most effective
work among Marquina's miscellaneous plays.[10] Both *Don Luis Mejía*
and *El estudiante endiablado (The Devilish Student)*, which is the
next work studied, are "costume dramas" and conceivably could
have been included among Marquina's historical plays. However,
both plays are directly inspired by specific literary works and thus
have a different character than dramas such as *The Sun Has Set in
Flanders* or even *Mountain Song* which was partially influenced by
writings of the Archpriest of Hita and the Marqués de Santillana.

   Don Luis Mejía is the same character who appears in José Zorrilla's *Don Juan Tenorio*. The original idea was Hernández Catá's
who proposed "writing a play about Don Luis Mejía, Tenorio's rival,
based on certain nuances of the psychology of both characters"
(*Works*,III,1357). According to Marquina, Hernández Catá had
pointed out that the antagonism between don Juan and don Luis
stems from the fact that don Juan does not fall in love with women
and don Luis does. "For don Juan Tenorio, his conquests are simply
a vital act; while for Mejía they are an affair of the heart"
(*Works*,III,1357).

   Act I takes place in Paris where don Luis steps out of his seducer's
role and altruistically helps the sick Clara de Lorena who is in love

with him. Act II is set in don Luis' house in Seville where four women arrive, one after the other. The first woman is a beggar with Clara's voice who convinces don Luis to shake hands with Molina, the man with whom he was about to duel. The second is Lucía, his fiancée's gypsy maid and with whom don Luis is "involved." The third is don Luis' mother who berates him for chasing after so many women and ignoring his fiancée, doña Ana de Pantoja. The latter arrives with the threatening news that don Juan has followed her to the house.

Don Luis discovers in Act III that don Juan has already seduced doña Ana, and he hires a boat to go to his adversary's estate. In the Epilogue which takes place next to don Juan's estate, the begger has a vision in which she sees don Luis die followed by her own death. The beggar reveals that she is really Clara. Once don Luis respected her and she is grateful. For that reason God allows him to choose. Clara tells don Luis that don Juan has killed him at dawn. If he accepts the hand she extends, he shall live. If he refuses, he will never return to the world. Don Luis does not accept and shortly thereafter is lifeless.

The play's originality stems from the authors having selected don Juan's adversary as their protagonist. José Zorrilla's *Don Juan Tenorio* concentrates essentially on the protagonist, while very little is learned about don Luis. Marquina and Hernández Catá's plan was to single out two aspects of don Luis' personal history: He falls in love and is don Juan's victim. One of don Luis' companions describes the first aspect: "He is not like don Juan, / whom all women chase / because there is not one he loves. / Don Luis loves them and is dying / to obtain more than they give; / . . . That is why women shall always belong to don Juan and don Luis to women" (*Works*, III, 1116). The second aspect is ably summed up by Díez-Canedo who states that don Luis "is subjected to fatality like a tragic hero. That fatality is embodied in don Juan Tenorio."[11]

Although don Juan never appears on stage, his presence, which drives don Luis toward death, is felt throughout the play. In Zorrilla's drama, don Juan is saved from damnation through the pure love he held for doña Inés. Don Luis, because of his altruistic act of helping Clara, has the option of saving himself by accepting her hand. He rejects it and dies. Manuel Pedro González pointed out what we consider to be the main flaw in don Luis' makeup: "During the entire play there is an obvious desire to reconcile two extremes, to humanize the professional seducer without weakening his lustful, bold, and fierce personality."[12] The play is generally well constructed, and the plot develops smoothly, although one notable exception is the lyrical effusion in which don Luis gives a long description of Seville. According to the reviews the play was well received.[13] Marquina has stated that *Don Luis Mejía* was "one of the greatest successes" in his "long theatrical life" (*Works*, III, 1359).

VIII   El estudiante endiablado (The Devilish Student)

Marquina wrote still another donjuanesque play, *The Devilish Student*, which was premièred in 1942.[14] *The Devilish Student* is based on José de Espronceda's *El estudiante de Salamanca (The Student at Salamanca)*, although the protagonist's ultimate salvation through love is borrowed from Zorrilla's *Don Juan Tenorio*. Espronceda's don Felix de Montemar is converted into another student at Salamanca, Rodrigo Pimentel. It is obvious from the very beginning that Marquina wants to save his protagonist who does not really possess the "satanic" quality of Espronceda's don Felix. Although Rodrigo takes part in a series of adventures and indulges in all kinds of blasphemies, Marquina's protective hand is visible. Pimentel's doña Inés is Teresa, and it is through his love for her that he is saved from both death and damnation.

The plot is hopelessly complicated and develops through countless situations and adventures. Nicolás González Ruiz has stated that *The Devilish Student* "has the appearance of being a new version of an old project. . . . It is a confused play, and certain versification defects, similar to those revealed by an earlier Marquina, make us lean toward the thesis of a reworking by the author of one of his first works."[15] Ironically enough the play enjoyed more than 100 performances, which was considerable for the times. The explanation, perhaps, is that Marquina was able to perceive that the type of escapist theater represented by *The Devilish Student* would be well received in 1942 when Spain was undergoing the difficult post-Civil War years.

CHAPTER 10

Poetry

I *Introduction*

IN 1900 Marquina published his first book, *Odas (Odes)*, a collection of poems previously published individually in the Barcelona
daily *La Publicidad*.[1] His most significant poetic works were to
appear during the next nine years, that is from *Odes* to *Canciones
del momento (Songs of the Moment)*, published in 1910. José Montero Alonso has traced the span of Marquina's poetry in the following terms:

With this last book [*Songs of the Moment*] his period as a lyric poet can be
considered closed. Starting in 1910 the theater will absorb almost all his
literary activity. Naturally it is not that he stopped composing verses
. . . but these verses, for the most part appear in response to the demands
of the particular moment. They are stanzas that have an immediate purpose:
to praise a city, toast a friend, give thanks. . . . Verses due to circumstances
and to the occasion rather than a voice spontaneously born.[2]

Our analysis of Marquina's poetry will concentrate on those works
written precisely during the period 1900–1910.

Marquina has generally been considered as one of Spain's Modernist poets.[3] Evidently he does share many points of contact with
Modernism such as the break with the poetry of the immediate past,
the search for new forms of poetic expression in language and meter,
and the melancholy air of some of his poems. However, he does not
share the affinity for dazzling images and the exotic and, at times,
decadent settings that characterize a great many Modernist poets.
Within Modernism, Marquina's poetry is relatively sober and contained, even prosaic at times, with an evident Classical influence
whose roots are very likely to be found in the author's humanistic

studies with the Jesuits. The very titles of some of his volumes of poetry seem to acknowledge this Classical influence: *Odes, Eglogas (Ecologues)*, and *Elegías (Elegies)*. This background in the classics, according to some critics, functioned as a check in Marquina's poetry on the freewheeling extravagances of Modernism.[4] Marquina's sociopolitical concerns and rebellious spirit, particularly manifest in *Odes*, would also seem to separate him from Modernism, essentially an aesthetic movement. The patriotic spirit of his poetry written after 1908, especially *Canciones del momento (Songs of the Moment)* published in 1910, has certain points of contact with the Generation of 98, although Marquina's habitual optimism is diametrically opposed to the pessimism prevalent among the writers of this group.

The rebellious spirit and sociopolitical concerns found in *Odes* have almost disappeared in *Ecologues* (published in 1902), to be replaced by love and nature, particularly the sea, as Marquina's basic thematic material.[5] The author has obviously begun to break away from the radicalism of his earlier works that he has called his "original sin" (*Works*, I, vii–xvi). There is also a significant toning down of the bombastic rhetoric of his first poems, a process continued in his next volume of poetry *Elegies* (published in 1905), in which love is the main theme. The year 1909 marks a high point in Marquina's poetry with the publication of *Vendimión*, his most ambitious and philosophical poetic composition, treating the struggle between time and the constant renewal of life. In 1910 the author's patriotic and civil themes make their appearance in *Songs of the Moment*, a thematic current also of *Tierras de España (Spanish Earth)* published in 1914. Both compositions, with his plays *The Daughters of the Cid, Doña María the Intrepid*, and *The Sun Has Set in Flanders*, mark Marquina's break with the rebellious spirit of his youth as he identifies himself in all these works with that Hispanic tradition which will be the leitmotiv of his future poems and dramas.

In the foregoing sketch of the most significant period of Marquina's poetry we have singled out only the predominant theme in each stage. However, it must be pointed out that many themes appear jointly in various compositions such as in *Odes* where, along with the author's idealized anarchism, we find poems such as "A una mujer" ("To a Woman") and "Cantar de las madres" ("Mothers' Song") in which the author extols the glories of motherhood. Other subsequent poetic works show Marquina as a poet of hearth and home as he sings the praises of family life and, at times, describes his reactions to his son's birth and growing up. Nature, a theme prevalent in his early compositions and the inspirational source of many early poetic images, appears infrequently after 1914.[6] After 1910 there is a gradual drift in Marquina's poetry toward orthodox religious topics as he draws away from the rebellious and pantheistic views of his youth. This inclination is already visible in *Spanish Earth* in 1914 and in compositions such as the long poem *San Francisco de Asís*, the author's collection of *Avisos y Máximas de Santa Teresa de Jesús (Advice and Maxims by Saint Teresa de Jesús)*, and the poems contained in *Lámparas (Lamps)*, published in 1927, 1942, and 1943 respectively. Marquina's preference for studying female characters in his theater has a comparable manifestation in the poems written over an extended period and published under the general title *Mujeres (1917–1936) (Women [1917–1936])* in Buenos Aires in 1936.

As does his theater, Marquina's poetry suffers from the author's overflowing versification. However, as he developed both his poetry and theater, the author gradually learned to control his verses and to lessen their rhetorical and declamatory tone.

II Odas (Odes)

Odes, a selection of poems published individually in the Barcelona daily *La Publicidad*, appeared in book form in 1900. The result is a heterogenous mixture of poems ranging from "Amargura" (Bitterness") to "Himno a la alegría" ("Hymn to Joy"). The main theme, however, is the author's rebellious spirit, and the general tone of the collection is one of nonconformity and alienation. Yet the optimism that was to characterize Marquina throughout his literary career is present in poems such as the aforementioned "Hymn to Joy" and especially "Brindis" ("A Toast") in which the poet sings the praises of a new life: "All await the new harvest/which together we are preparing."; "Todos esperan la cosecha nueva,/la que nosotros preparando estamos" (*Works*,VI,81).

In *Odes* (as in Marquina's first play *The Shepherd* which has a similar focus), the ideology is not clearly defined. The author seems to view himself in both works as a sort of Messianic spokesman who

proposes an idealized anarchism that aspires to a Utopian state. Juan
Valera used *Odes* as a point of departure for an article entitled "La
irresponsibilidad de los poetas y la purificación de la poesía" ("The
Irresponsibility of Poets and the Purification of Poetry") in which
the literary elder statesman praised the young poet's ability but at
the same time chided his Utopian views: "Apocalyptic bard, he
threatens with destruction and death, ruin and fire, the institutions,
the altars, and the thrones of all that stands on the face of the
earth. . . . What will come after the predicted radical revolution is
confusedly discernible . . . through the symbols and colossal images and in the allegorical figures created and displayed by the poet.
It seems that there no longer will be Pope, nor king, nor bishops,
nor judges, nor priests. Each of us will be our own Pope, king,
judge, and priest. . . . Humanity shall be happy and live in deli-
cious anarchy and on perpetual strike."[7]
    Marquina's hoped-for world had as its basis the concept of man in
a primitive natural state, free from contamination by the "civilized"
world. As outlined above by Juan Valera, *Odes* reveals a Marquina
who advocated destruction of society along with all that had been
fabricated by man. Nature, however, is preserved by the author as
he extols mountains, rocks, and the sea. In the poem "El padre
caos" ("Father Chaos") the author praises the harmony of nature
vis-à-vis the chaos of the man-made world — (*Works*, IV, 73–77) —
and in "La voz del torrente" ("The Voice of the Torrent"), the mountain torrent passes unfettered past the "ruins of castles and
churches" — symbols of the destruction of temporal and religious
power (*Works*, VI, 40–41). This last theme is repeated with variations
in "El templo en ruinas" ("The Temple in Ruins") (*Works*, VI, 33–
35). In the last poem, "Crisis," Marquina indicates that man in a
previous period shut himself off from a natural life. Man now wishes
to return to that life but is passing through a crisis as in his attempts
to return he finds himself in an intermediate state.

III   Las vendimias (The Grape Harvests)

    Marquina's next poetic compositon after *Odes* was *Las vendimias*
(The Grape Harvests), published in 1901. Whereas *Odes* was a collection of disparate poems, *The Grape Harvests* is a work that has a

unified structure and theme. The poem is divided into three parts:
"El día de las viñas ("The Day of the Vineyards"), "El día del lagar"
("The Day of the Wine Press"), and "El día del misterio" ("The Day
of the Mystery").

In "The Day of the Vineyards," Marquina equates the work of the
grape harvest to a religious ritual which represents the life process.
The author invites all in the vineyards "to celebrate the mass of
life/on the green altars"; "a celebrar la misa de la vida/sobre las aras
verdes" (*Works*,VI,88). Throughout the poem Marquina's pantheism that had begun to appear in *Odes* becomes more evident. While
"The Day of the Vineyards" takes place during the morning, "The
Day of the Wine Press" develops during the midday hour and the
siesta, that is when the sun, which represents the power of nature,
is at its zenith. In the poem "Canción del sol" ("Song of the Sun") the
author pictures this celestial body in all its splendor. "The Day of
the Mystery" takes place during the twilight hour during which the
poet meditates on the enigma of life. He directs the poem "Las siete
palabras del poeta" ("The Seven Words of the Poet") to an impatient
and suspicious humanity: "You have pained me, Humanity that
cries/around the press, as if the wine/would not be made;" ("Me has
dado pena, Humanidad, que gritas/en torno del lagar, como si el
vino/no se hubiera de hacer;" (*Works*,VI,122). The seven words are:
"Patience," "Strength," "Perserverance," "Assertion," "Serenity,"
"Generosity," and "Beauty." In this poem, Marquina's pantheism
does not focus on Nature's force from an exterior point of view, for
example, with a description of the monumental aspect of the mountains or the power of the sea; rather, he concerns himself with what
he considers the inherent laws of natural evolution. These are fixed
laws of birth and destruction which are exemplified by the grape
that is destroyed in the must and which reaches full realization when
it becomes wine. Despite singling out one element such as the
grape and the creation of wine, Marquina's pantheism is related to a
more universal concept. Men and women, young and old join in the
grape harvest as a collective task. It is a total brotherhood composed
of man and nature that carries out a ritual conceived in marked
religious terms.

The epilogue of the first edition of *The Grape Harvests* reveals the
young Marquina's social concerns. The author indicates that *The
Grape Harvests* is the first of a series of Georgic poems that he plans

to work on during his youth and explains their background as follows:

A general feeling serves as a link between all these poems: the deep love I
have for all work related to the earth, a love that has gained in strength
within me and has become almost a religion through the study — still
rather rudimentary — of the labor problem. Next to the immorality and
injustice of the factories and workshops . . . that enslave the man of the
city, I see developing grandly and solemnly the poem of work in the fields, a
faithful continuation of Nature's work. . . . When the earth, that dark slave
of the privileged, belongs to all and we cultivate it in peace, the labor
problem will be resolved.[8]

IV Eclogues and Elegies

Eclogues, written in 1902, was Marquina's next poetic composition. The author states in the notes included in his complete works
that the title *Eclogues* does not refer to bucolic poems but rather to
the "etymological sense of the word (in Greek *ekloge* 'extract,
selected piece')" because the poems included in the volume "had
their origin in a more or less minute and careful selection" from
among his compositions (*Works*, VI, 1300). In *Eclogues* Marquina's
poetry is clearly in a transitional state. There are still traces of the
rebellious author who wrote *Odes* in "Balada de los golfos" ("Ballad
of the Vagabonds"), but other poems point toward another, still
undefined, direction such as the "Epilogue" subtitled "Invocación a
octubre" ("Invocation of October"). Here the barely twenty-three-
year-old author selects the autumnal season in order to meditate and
question — somewhat rhetorically — the meaning of life (*Works*,
VI, 159).[9] These compositions have more the tone of an elderly poet
looking back reflectively on a long life than of the young author who
only two years before had published *Odes*. This new direction will
eventually lead to Marquina's definite break with the rebellious
spirit of his youth, as he identifies more fully with the Hispanic
tradition.

Marquina has stated in the notes cited that *Eclogues* has "two
concrete themes, that of a distinct woman, with whom we speak at
times and of whom some gestures and attitudes are devotedly reproduced, and that of the sea, which now appears for the first time

as a living reality . . . bathing with Mediterranean unction the poet's soul" (*Works*, VI, 1300). The woman referred to is apparently Mercedes Pichot, whom Marquina married on June 18, 1903, and who probably was the inspirational source behind the love poems included in *Eclogues* and *Elegies*. The main theme in *Eclogues* is clearly love and not the sea, although the latter figures prominently in many poems. Often both themes appear in the same composition, since, as we shall shortly see, through love Marquina gains a greater understanding of nature, and particularly of the sea.

In *Eclogues* the author is no longer placing his hopes for man's salvation in social vindication, but rather beginning to find it in love. This new-found faith, which becomes manifest in his next volume of poetry, *Elegies*, is evident in Eclogue V as the poet directs himself to the woman he loves: "What to do, what to do without you, Guardian of mine?/ You, my support, you the only resting place/in so desperate a struggle!" ("¿Qué hacer, qué hacer sin ti, Custodia mía?/ Tú mi sostén, tú el único descanso/en tan desesperada lucha!") (*Works*, VI, 140).

Marquina has imbued his poetry in *Eclogues* with a mysterious air. In this respect Federico de Onís has stated the following:

This youthful love has a mystic religious background. The love of a woman is the light of life that illuminates all things; that is why through the sentiment of love, Marquina's poetry gives us a deep feeling of nature, men, and life. At the beginning, when there is no love . . . all things that surround the young poet produce a feeling of mystery. . . . When love arrives, not only is his soul transfigured, but also all that surrounds him is transfigured, illuminated, and he discovers its hidden and true meaning. Disquiet is converted into serenity, into plenitudes, into the healthy joy of living. This is the distance that exists between *Eclogues* and *Elegies*.[10]

This power of love is displayed in Eclogue XII titled "Nacimiento" ("Birth"):

Said the son to the father:
"All is futile father;
my sadness is deeper
than the depth of the valley. . . ."

Decía al padre el hijo:
"Todo es inútil padre;
mi tristeza es más honda
que la hondura del valle. . . ."
(*Works*, VI, 149)

However, love enters his life, and the same things that saddened him before, now fill him with happiness: "All is beautiful father;/my joy sweeter/than the fog of the valley. . . ." "Todo es hermoso padre;/mi alegría, más dulce/que las nieblas del valle . . ." (Works, VI,150).

Marquina has noted that the themes in *Eclogues* begin to "put order in the turbulence and profuse declamation found in *Odes*" (Works,VI,1300). There is a toning down with respect to Marquina's previous poems; however, his declamatory style is still very much in evidence. Although the themes have changed, the poetic language both in *Eclogues* and *Elegies* is essentially the same. As in previous works, Marquina depends excessively on a limited vocabulary drawn from nature: words such as rocks, waves, seas, mountains, and trees are constantly repeated.

The theme of love that had been gradually gaining in importance since Marquina's first poems is all-encompassing in *Elegies*, as it is the work's only theme. As in *Eclogues*, the title is misleading, since only in the last part of the volume do Marquina's verses acquire a tone of lament. The opening verses seem to indicate that the author had recently undergone a trying experience, as he rejoices at his again finding the poetic word: "Again I sing, and to me it is resurrection./ . . . The saddened soul, smiles again. . . ." ("Vuelvo a cantar, y me es resurrección/ . . . El alma, triste, vuelve a sonreír . . .") (Works,VI,163). These verses are probably alluding to the fact that no volume of Marquina's verses appeared between the years that separate *Eclogues* from *Elegies*, published in 1902 and 1905 respectively. This sudden decrease in poetic production for reasons not made clear by the author stands in contrast to the period 1900–1902 which saw the publication of *Odes*, *The Grape Harvests*, and *Eclogues*.

During this hiatus the poet of *Odes* has undergone a marked spiritual transformation. In *Elegies* Marquina searches for direct, simple communication, as his poetry acquires a confessional, intimate character. At times, his poems are so personal that communication is hindered. Unamuno in a letter to Marquina noted this particular aspect of *Elegies:* "Your poetry is too intimate for our people that are raised in the streets. . . . Besides the poems are not declamable. I congratulate you on them . . . for not having thought of those who were going to read them."[11] Marquina had announced in an earlier letter to Unamuno that he was preparing *Elegies* which he hoped would erase in the latter's memory "the loud sonorities" of his "early rhymed eloquence."[12] In spite of his declared intent, Marquina failed to rid his poetry of the rhetoric so prominent in his previous compositions. Unamuno in the same letter indicates that at times Marquina lets "his rhyme carry him away."

Elegies is one long, perhaps too long, canto dedicated to love. The poet's prime purpose is to communicate the exaltation he feels because of love, though as we have noted, at times Marquina's effusions are lost on the reader because the poems are too directly related to his personal experience. The poet finds in love the desired sense of security and serenity referred to in our analysis of *Eclogues:* "Let time go forward, run and consume itself,/for love and spring have carried me/to the quiet security of the eternal!" "¡Avance, corra y se deshaga el tiempo,/que amor y primavera me han llevado a la quietud segura de lo eterno!" (*Works*,VI,185). Through love the mysteries of the universe are explained to the poet who states "that at my side is love,/key that opens worlds/chariot that takes me to the sun." ("que está a mi lado el amor,/llave que me abre los mundos,/carro que me lleva al sol" (*Works*,VI,165). The title *Elegies* is better understood during the last part of the work as Marquina in a series of poems expresses his suffering because the perfect love he has experienced does not extend itself to the entire universe:

Oh! I do not lament attaining love;	¡Oh! ¡No me quejo del amor logrado;
ingratitude will not stain my verse;	no ha de manchar la ingratitud mi verso;
my lament is not seeing it realized, at each instant, in all the Universe!	quéjome de no verlo realizado, a cada instante en todo el Universo!

(*Works*,VI,217)

V Vendimión

Between 1907 and 1908 Marquina wrote *Vendimión*, the most ambitious and philosophical of all his poetic compositions. Published in 1909, *Vendimión* is a long poem projected on a sweeping and grandiose scale.[13] In a letter to Unamuno announcing the near-complete *Vendimión*, Marquina states that it is "a series of lucubrations in verse dealing with time and death from all the fundamental sentiments of my personality."[14] Gómez de Baquero has singled out the poem's focus: "Vendimión is time, considered as a principle of destruction. 'Oh time, Vendimión of all grape harvests!' The poem is a myth of the struggle between time and the eternal renewal of life, between destruction and creation."[15] For Marquina life itself is a constant renewal.

It must be noted that at times *Vendimión* becomes rather muddled as Marquina loses himself in complex and imprecise theorizing, although we would not go as far as Gómez de Baquero who, while praising the "richness and variety" of its elements, states that the poem is "disorganized, confused, and almost chaotic."[16] Vendimión is a name apparently invented by Marquina, possibly combining the words *vendimia* ("grape harvest") and *demonio* ("devil"). As we have noted in our study of *Las vendimias (The Grape Harvests)*, the gathering of grapes represents for Marquina the life process. Vendimión who at times is personified, appears in "Vendimión ermitaño" ("Vendimion the Hermit") as a bearded man with diabolic characteristics. In describing his composite personality Marquina states that he is both "friar and devil" (*Works*,VI,479).

In *Vendimión*, the author displays his imaginative ability at its best. The poem's complex content includes various plots, myths, legends, fables, figures out of Spain's history, and even Dante. These multiple and varied parts are drawn together by Marquina's concern with the struggle between time and the constant renewal of life. In the first part of the work Vendimión pantheistically disintegrates to form the world out of a nebulous state. Once disintegrated, Vendimión becomes time, and all things participate in his essence. Marquina who identifies himself as an "Hispanic-Latin bard" initiates a struggle with Vendimión to combat time's destruction of the poetic word:

But my voice, my perennial
    voice, of infinite
virtue, in the sacredness of
    the written word,
when my tongue is silenced,
    when they are crying
    over me
in my home, my voice will
    continue to respond.
	Pero mi voz, perenne,
	    de infinita
	virtud, en el sagrado de la
	    palabra escrita,
	cuando mi lengua calle, cuando
	    me estén llorando
	
	en mi casa, mi voz seguirá
	    resonando.

(*Works*,VI,435)

Toward this end Marquina finds inspiration in three creatures: the ass, the swan, and the eagle who symbolize respectively work, love — presented through the Greek myth of Leda — and creative strength:[17]

Vendimión destroyer: so that your	Vendimión destructor: para que el rayo
lightning does not annihilate me	tuyo no me aniquile
in the tragic storm,	en la tormenta trágica
I shall live as the donkey,	viviré como el asno,
love as the swan,	amaré como el cisne,
create as the eagle.	crearé como el ágila.

(*Works*, VI, 471)

In "Vendimión the Hermit", presented within the structure of a prayer book called "Libro de horas" ("Book of Hours"), Vendimión, or time, appears, as the title implies, disguised as a hermit. He speaks to the poet of life and eternity and defends death as a final resting place. This is the most lyrical part of the entire composition; Marquina envelops Vendimión and the poet in a supernatural and mysterious atmosphere. The poet deals with the passage of time and its effect on marriage in "Vendimión doméstico" ("Domestic Vendimión"). Once the initial bliss of marriage has passed, the couple, particularly the wife, begins to feel resentment born of boredom. The marriage begins to die since no event has occurred to renew it. The birth of a son produces the miracle of renewal. Time has been overcome: "And that one, with the sour gesture,/that I call Vendimión, flees defeated." ("Y aquel del agrio gesto,/que llamo Vendimión, huye vencido") (*Works*, VI, 525).

In "Vendimión hispánico" ("Hispanic Vendimión") Marquina — who in his future works will defend the Hispanic tradition — deals in the section titled "En la historia" ("In History") with the struggle between the "historical tradition, between all that time makes old and decrepit, and the spirit of renewal."[18] Marquina's representatives of this spirit are three widely different historical characters: The Cid, don Alvaro de Luna, and Juan de Padilla. All three are presented as exalted figures vis-à-vis their respective kings who represent "historical tradition." Charles I is particularly censured by Marquina as the *comunero* Padilla struggles against the monarch's absolutism.

In the last part of the poem "Vendimión astral" ("Astral Vendimión") Marquina sums up his conclusions as he addresses Humanity:

Eternity, not time, is your quadrant;	La eternidad no el tiempo es tu cuadrante;
now not death, but God is before you;	ya no a la muerte, a Dios tienes delante;
. . . .	. . . .
The works we do today, for the future are destined;	Las obras que hoy hacemos, ya a los futuros tiempos las movemos;
the church we found to unborn God is destined.	la iglesia que fundamos a Dios que no ha nacido destinamos.
Thus we place in savage death for attainment and plentitude our ideal;	Así ponemos en la muerte fiera a logro y plenitud nuestra quimera;
and if we die in our attempt, in our interminable work we live on.	y si en ella morimos, en la obra interminable persistimos.

(*Works*, VI, 641)

Thus in order to "defeat time and death, Humanity should put in
its works a concept of eternity, to work *sub specie aeterni*."[19]

VI   Canciones del momento (Songs of the Moment)

Songs of the Moment, published in 1910, is a collection of poems
that had originally appeared in the newspaper *Heraldo de Madrid*
under the same title. These compositions are Marquina's lyrical
commentaries on events and themes of the times and were written
during 1908 and 1909. Although *Songs of the Moment* contains some
widely varying works such as "Elogio de Holanda en el nacimiento
de una princesa" ("In Praise of Holland on the Birth of a Princess")
and "Ricardo Wagner," most of the poems deal with Spain and
reveal the author's patriotic and civic spirit. The opening poem
entitled "Estrofas votivas" ("Votive Stanzas") reveals the *leitmotiv*
both of *Songs of the Moment* and of Marquina's future literary production when the poet directs himself to his son:

On your crib of ancient boards, that will be my sepulture if I lie;	Sobre tu cuna de tablas antiguas, que me serán sepultura si miento;

son born in the ambiguous nights	hijo nacido en las noches ambiguas
of disasters and defeat,	de los desastres y del vencimiento,
. . . .	. . . .
curse me if I should die	maldíceme si llego a la muerte
without singing a song of the Spanish race!	sin entonar un canto de raza!

(*Works*,VI,301)

In the prologue to his complete works, dated April 28, 1944, Marquina has singled out the importance of these verses in his spiritual development, along with the patriotic dedication of *The Daughters of the Cid* and his prayer of faith to the Virgin in his volume of poetry *Spanish Earth* (*Works*,VI,763) published in 1914: "Spain in body and soul; love of God in His divine mother: see here the sense of these three cries. The three flow together in a straight road of salvation. And although on occasion, the dust of time has dirtied my sandals, I can swear that since then, thirty long years of poetry and work have not seen me knowingly stray from what I believed to be the good path" (*Works*,I,xv). Marquina indicates that these "three cries" represent his break with the "temporal stigma" which is the "original sin" of an author: "The days tell a writer the ideas of his time in the manner and style or mode of his time. Temporal ideas and style: substance and form of his original sin . . ." (*Works*,I,x). Marquina does not really define his particular "temporal stigma" but does vaguely indicate that it was "liberalism" (*Works*,I,xii).

Federico de Onís has stated that Marquina's *Songs of the Moment* attempt to search out "the national meaning" of contemporary events as he "views them from the perspective of an interpretation of the past and an ideal of the future, characteristic of the man of 1898."[20] In these poems there are numerous points of contact with the Generation of 1898: the influence of the disastrous war with the United States, the preoccupation with a defeated Spain after the disaster, and the interest in Castille as a source of inspiration and hope. However, most poems in *Songs of the Moment* treating Spain lack the critical perspective adopted by the writers of 1898 toward their country. In addition, Marquina's habitual optimism sets him apart from the pessimism generally attributed to the aforementioned generation.

Many of the patriotic poems in *Songs of the Moment* are of the

122 EDUARDO MARQUINA

flag-waving variety, such as "Patria" ("Motherland"), where Marquina incites his country to rise up and soar like the eagle from the past toward the future. In the same poem Marquina suggests author, works, and country have become one: "Because you also are in me; my work/motherland you annoint with sublime unction. . . ." ("Porque también tú estás en mí; mis obras,/patria, las unges de tu unción excelsa . . . ") (*Works*,VI,337). In "Cien años después" ("One Hundred Years After"), the centennial of the Spanish uprising against the French on May 2, 1808 causes Marquina to reflect on his defeated country's second-rate status on the world scene. Although the poet himself is happy with the simple things in Spain, for others he would like his nation to regain her past glories:

That your banner be raised as before, with its castles, imperial, and that your voice be for the enemy leaders a hangman's noose.	Que tu estandarte se alzara, como antes, con sus castillos, imperial, y que tu voz fuese, para los enemigos caudillos un dogal.

(*Works*,VI,319)

The author's faith in the future of his country is affirmed in "Castilla labradora" ("Agricultural Castile"). Written on the occasion of an agricultural conference of Castilian farmers, the poet finds inspiration and hope in the fields of Castile, symbol of the entire nation (*Works*,VI,346–48). With "Ramo de olivo" ("Olive Branch") Marquina marks the warm welcome given Spanish sailors upon their arrival in Havana for the first time after the war of 1898 (*Works*,VI,326–28). In "Plegaria" ("Prayer") written on April 14, 1909, Marquina approaches the attitude of the men of 1898 as he adopts a critical attitude toward Spain and her problem:

Look, mother Spain, there is no waiting when the hungry beg with eagerness; notice that your race, pale and austere, begs for science and letters. . . .	Mira, madre España, que no tiene espera el hambriento cuando pide con afán; mira que tu raza, pálida y austera pide ciencia y letras. . . .

(*Works*,VI,383)

Marquina the civic poet is in evidence in many poems. "Elogio de Carlos III" ("In Praise of Charles III") is the poet's testimonial to the eighteenth-century monarch whom he describes as a "great Spaniard, great king, and great citizen." The poem's inspiration is the many projects undertaken in Madrid by Charles III during his reign (*Works*, VI,352–54). Another poem in this vein is "Ofrenda" ("Offering") in which Marquina, on the occasion of the "Conference of the Press" held in Madrid in 1908, extols the civic role of journalism.

Marquina has adapted his poetic style to the newspaper readers for whom the compositions in *Songs of the Moment* were originally written. The language is direct, simple, quite often prosaic, without complications of any type. The poems are worlds apart in language, ideology, and style from *Vendimión* (written around the same time). *Songs of the Moment* is significant because it signals Marquina's break with his rebellious youth and initiates, along with his dramas produced during the years 1908–1910, the main theme of his future literary production: Spain and the Hispanic tradition.

VII Recogimiento (Sanctuary)

The collection of poems entitled *Sanctuary*, which was not published until it appeared in Marquina's complete works, is the best and most significant of the author's later poetic works. These compositions, written between 1917 and 1926, differ from the rest of Marquina's poetic works in that they are totally intimate, intended more for the poet himself than for publication. The author of *Sanctuary* reveals himself as a poet free of excess lyrical ornamentation, expressing feelings inspired by personal events. The tone and focus of *Sanctuary* is set in the opening verses: "I call myself to confession/in a low voice. . . ." ("Me llamo a confesión/a mí mismo en voz baja . . . ") (*Works*,VI,971). The poems are expressed with great tenderness and dignity and are not at all maudlin. We see a totally different Marquina, no longer surrounded by the seas, mountains, and trees of earlier works. His habitual optimism is noticeably absent, particularly in the first part where the poet reflects on themes of the soul, death, and eternity. Perhaps the best poem of the entire collection is "La visitante" ("The Visitor") in which Marquina has a conversation with his soul, who appears before his door

as a strange figure "unknown and sad, very sad" (*Works*, VI, 976). All
the poems in the first part are enveloped in an atmosphere of silent
voices, late afternoons, and twilight hours. We are light years away
from the declamatory Marquina observed in earlier poems. The
second part, "El padre y el hijo" ("Father and Son"), is devoted to
poems inspired by his son's growing up.[21] *Sanctuary* closes with a
poem titled "Nueva flor" ("New Flower") dedicated to his grand-
daughter born on May 8, 1926.

Sanctuary and *Vendimión* indicated two directions for the possible future development of Marquina's poetry. *Vendimión*, with its
cosmic perspective and prophetic, albeit still rough-hewn, poetic
voice, suggested an original area of exploitation for Marquina's
muse. *Sanctuary*, with its lyrical sincerity and the bare, personal
confession free of grandiloquence and rhetoric, offers ample proof
that Marquina had the potential to be a significant cultivator of this
intimate type of poetry. The poetic potential evident in these works
was truncated because Marquina devoted most of his energies to the
theater after 1910. His poems written after 1910, as noted in the
introduction, were inspired more by immediate circumstances than
by an authentic lyrical voice. Marquina also chose to emphasize the
Hispanic tradition in works such as *Spanish Earth* and *Los tres libros
de España (The Three Books of Spain)*. These factors drew Marquina away from the types of themes that had inspired *Vendimión*
and *Sanctuary* and consequently did not allow the development of a
significant body of the type of poetic compositions for which he was
perhaps best suited.

CHAPTER 11

Novels and Stories

I Introduction

THE least-known aspect of Marquina's literary production is his novels and short stories. Critics have generally ignored these works. Occasionally a passing reference is made to the fact that Marquina, in addition to poetry and dramas, also wrote novels and short stories. These works have not influenced the development of narrative prose, and Marquina is included in histories of Spanish literature because of his theater and poetry. After 1910, he very likely did not think of himself as a novelist or short story writer. From 1910, when he definitely established himself on the Spanish stage, Marquina devoted his energies almost entirely to the theater, writing prose fiction only occasionally, and even less frequently after 1920.

Marquina published his first narratives in *El cuento semanal* (*The Weekly Story*). This magazine, founded in 1907 by Eduardo Zamacois, was extremely important in popularizing the short narrative at the turn of the century. Many important novelists were able to get their start through this weekly.[1] Some issues went through several printings and reached a circulation of 100,000.[2] Many other collections of the same type followed in the wake of *The Weekly Story* such as *La novela semanal* (*The Weekly Novel*) and *La novela corta* (*The Short Novel*) in 1921 and 1916 respectively. Zamacois himself founded another similar magazine in 1909, *Los contemporáneos* (*The Contemporaries*), to which Marquina continued to contribute.

Marquina s novels and stories generally have a realistic setting and style — noteworthy in itself, given the lyric character of the rest of his literary production.[3] This is due, perhaps, to the fact that Marquina was adapting himself to the taste of *The Weekly Story*

whose contributors included numerous realistic writers; he probably perceived also that there was little market for poetic narratives.
However, many of Marquina's novels and stories parallel the development of his contemporary plays, practically all written in prose
with themes, characters, and realistic settings similar to his narrative works. Indeed, in one of the stories, *Maternidad (Motherhood)*,
we find characters, Pilar and Carmen Astorga, who also appear in
his contemporary play, *One Woman*. There are, of course, narratives with a lyrical character, but these are a minority.[4] Interestingly
enough, the most outstanding of all his narratives is the novel,
Almas anónimas (Anonymous Souls), which because of its lyrical
quality could, perhaps, best be described as a prose poem.
Anonymous Souls suggests that Marquina's talent lay in creating
works in which his lyric muse could operate freely, and not in the
conventional, realistic style of most of his narratives.

    His stories and novels generally have a contemporary urban set-
ting. Notably absent are those settings far away in time and place
that characterize his theater. There are only two historical narratives
in his *Complete Works:* the novel *La reina mujer (The Queen is a
Woman Too)* and the short story *El reverso de la medalla (The Other
Side of the Medal)*, both of which have characters that also appear in
his plays: In the former work, the Catholic monarchs and in the latter,
Benvenuto Cellini. The rural setting, prominent in his theater, appears only in the short story, *Como las abejas (Like the Bees)*. Most
of Marquina's narratives take place in Spain, although earlier ones
written for *The Weekly Story* are set in other parts of Europe, i.e.,
London, Brussels, and particularly Paris. The predominance of
Spanish settings after this early stage is perhaps related to Marquina's identification with the Hispanic tradition after 1908. It must be
pointed out, however, that the patriotic exaltation characteristic of
his historical dramas is absent in his novels and stories.

    The author's narrative technique is conventional and makes slight
demands on his readers. His narratives generally follow a uniform
chronological order and function on only one level. At times there
are flashbacks, or two actions that develop at different times as in
Las dos vidas (Two Lives) or *Almas anónimas (Anonymous Souls)*,
but Marquina is always there to elucidate and explain. Both novels
and stories are narrated generally in the third person by an impersonal, all-knowing author. However, quite often the author directs
himself to his reader — e.g., "as my readers already know . . ."

— to clear up a point or as a guide. At times he will use a first person narrator, either as impersonal witness to the events as in *La 'muestra' (The 'Sample')*, or narrate via a main character such as the doctor in *El destino cruel (Cruel Destiny)*. Quite often the all-knowing author appears himself, and relates incidents his first person narrators have not observed. In three stories, *Rosas de sangre (Blood Roses)*, *Un niño malo (A Bad Boy)*, and *El reverso de la medalla (The Other Side of the Medal)*, Marquina reverts to the convention aptly used by Cervantes of a "story within a story": the narrator claims to find some papers that contain the events he is reproducing for the reader. A variation on this technique is offered in *The Other Side of the Medal* in which Benvenuto Cellini presents the Duque of Cosme a portion of his still-to-be-completed autobiography. The Duke's reading of Cellini's writings form the basis of this "story within a story." The author further attempts to aid the reader by dividing just about all his narratives into brief chapters, each with a Roman numeral, and by adding an epilogue in which he neatly ties together all loose ends.[5]

Marquina is a much better short story writer than novelist. The four novels included in his complete works *Anonymous Souls, Two Lives, El beso en la herida (Balm on the Wound)*, and *The Queen is a Woman Too* seem rather overdeveloped and somewhat "wordy" short stories, particularly the last two. Usually his stories include only one basic action, and Marquina handles it without difficulty. However, in a novel such as *The Queen is a Woman Too* which is rather complicated in that Marquina must contend with various parallel actions, the author's awkwardness becomes quite evident as he attempts to maintain coordination between the different component parts.

Love and the difficult path a woman must tread to achieve it remain, as in his theater, is a favorite theme. There is, however, less emphasis on his formula of confronting two women who represent "good" and "bad" love respectively with the inevitable triumph of the former. In stories such as *Adán y Eva en el 'Dancing' (Adam and Eve in the Dance Hall)* and *El secreto de la vida (The Secret of Life)* there is concern for the effects of modern times on people's ability to love. In four stories grouped under the title *Almas de mujer (Women's Souls)* the author studies the effects of the "transitional times," in which the author lives, on the female psyche. Marquina's social preoccupation, evident in the early plays and poems, is almost com-

pletely absent in his narratives. The only vestige of the author's
youthful radicalism is a romanticized anarchist in the story *La
caravana (The Caravan)* published in 1907. There is perhaps a social
theme within the framework of the story *Fin de raza (End of a Race)*
where an aristocratic family gains new strength through the son's
marriage to a maid.

Whereas Marquina's theater is characterized by the dominance of
female protagonists, in his narratives there are almost as many principal male characters as female. This would seem to confirm what
we have indicated in our study of Marquina's theater: many of his
plays were conceived as vehicles for the female actresses — María
Guerrero, Margarita Xirgu, and Lola Membrives — who dominated the Spanish stage during the first part of the twentieth century. The fact that these "stars" were not a consideration in his
narratives perhaps prompted Marquina to try his hand at creating
male characters. The results indicate that regardless of the genre,
the author was better at creating female characters.[6]

II   *The Novels*

Anonymous Souls, the first novel included in Marquina's complete works is, as we have indicated, both his most lyrical and best
prose work, perhaps best described as a prose poem. Although the
author utilized a basic plot familiar in his theater, that of two women
who compete for the love of the same man, he has imbued *Anonymous Souls* with an evocative poetic melancholy on an artistic par
with his best poems and plays. Compared to the rest of his narratives, *Anonymous Souls* is ample proof that Marquina functioned at
his best in a poetic vein.

Set in a Spanish coastal village, *Anonymous Souls*, published in
1909, is the love story of Agueda Pía and the Italian architect, Marco
Fortis. Agueda Pía is the embodiment of goodness and the sense of
sacrifice that Marquina exalts in his idealized female protagonists.
She is another of the author's heroines who offers man a source of
tranquility amid life's trials and tribulations. Rather than a lover she
is a mother figure, as noted in plays such as *Benvenuto Cellini* and
The White Monk. Marco Fortis, who felt incapable of loving,
learned to do so through Agueda Pía. Yet Agueda Pía in the process

sacrificed her own love as Marco, who had always felt an attraction for the Italian Countess Monica, but was unable to understand his feelings, returned to the Countess. The work ends on a bitter sweet note as Agueda Pía understands and forgives Marco Fortis. The characters are drawn rather sketchily as Marquina places more emphasis in *Anonymous Souls* on poetic climate, the work's most notable aspect, than on delineation.

In his next two novels, *Two Lives* and *Balm on the Wound*, published in 1919 and 1920 respectively, Marquina again employs his basic plot of placing two women, one representing "good" love and the other "bad" love in competition for the love of the same man. In *Two Lives*, set partly in Paris and partly in Spain, the protagonist Pedro Morales finally realizes that his young and "good" sister-in-law Laurette is the woman he really loves rather than his adulterous wife, Maguí. *Balm on the Wound* has a variation on the basic plot with no automatic triumph of "good" love over "bad." The protagonist Irene Pombal, another of Marquina's heroines who are goodness incarnate, rejects the man she has always loved, Miguel Arenal, after the latter's wife, the "bad" Clara Montoro, has died. Irene Pombal's delineation is the most interesting feature in these two novels. Marquina has given her a tragic, melancholic air which recalls one of his best characterizations, Deseada, the protagonist of his rural drama, *The Hermitage, the Fountain, and the River*. Both novels are long and "wordy," as if Marquina wished to take advantage of the wider scope offered to him by his novels over his stories.

In *The Queen Is a Woman Too*, the last novel included in Marquina's *Complete Works*, the author studies the personality of the Catholic Queen Isabella, whom he greatly admired and who appeared in two of his plays, *The Flowers of Aragón* and *The Great Captain*.[7] Although Marquina managed generally to control his poetic muse and develop his novel in a realistic style, at times he waxes lyrical when extolling the figure of the Queen or the vast undertaking of the Catholic monarchs in the New World. The novel is his most complex narrative. Marquina handles various separate actions dealing with Columbus' efforts to outfit his expedition, Ferdinand's problems arising from his extramarital affairs, Ferdinand and Isabella together and Isabella acting alone. *The Queen Is a Woman Too* is burdened with incidents and numerous digressions. It is evident from Marquina's somewhat awkward attempts to relate and coordinate these actions that, although the novel was written in 1941 toward the end of his career, he still lacked the talent to develop so ambitious a narrative smoothly.

Isabella is the author's main concern as he evokes the figure of the Catholic Queen. The play's title indicates the tone of Marquina's delineation of Isabella: *The Queen Is a Woman Too*. In this respect Isabella states: "All my science is geared to remaining a woman, I govern my kingdom as other women their homes" (*Works*, VII, 513). Marquina emphasizes the love of Isabella for Ferdinand and the jealousy she felt because of his extramarital affairs. "She serves Spain, trusts in God, governs her house, and adores Ferdinand" (*Works*, VII, 444). His admiration of the Queen leads him to defend Isabella's establishing the Inquisition in Spain. Ferdinand is an intelligent and capable ruler; however, next to the idealized and exalted figure of the Queen he comes out second best.[8]

III   *The Stories*

The Caravan, published in 1907, is the most interesting of Marquina's early stories. It deals with the impossible love between the opera singer, la Buzzi, and the Russian anarchist-activist, Ivanoff, both of whom are "two travelers in a restless caravan that across the world . . . continues tò search for a Mecca wherein to pay homage to their ideal" (*Works*, VII, 884). The anarchist is the story's most noteworthy feature. He is the last link to Marquina's early rebellious spirit which was to change the following year with the author's identification with the "establishment" in Spain. Although Marquina does not idealize the anarchist, he does picture him quite sympathetically and surrounds him with a Romantic aura. Ivanoff dies in Brussels as a bomb he carried, intended for the Royal Palace, explodes prematurely. It is interesting to observe that Marquina was one of the first to publish in *The Weekly Story* as *The Caravan* appeared in February 1907, the same year the magazine was founded.

In *El secreto de la vida* (*The Secret of Life*) and *Adán y Eva en el 'Dancing'* (*Adam and Eve in the 'Dance Hal'*), written in 1909 and 1926 respectively, Marquina manifests his preoccupation with the modern world's effect on people's ability to love. *The Secret of*

Life takes place in the twenty-fifth century. There are no problems for the wise men of this century (called·"psychologists"), and electrical energy, supplied in unlimited quantity to all, has erased material needs. These changes were contrary to man's instinct of reproduction, called in previous centuries by the poetic name of "love," and humanity began to decline. However, the psychologist Smith in London announces he has found a fluid that will change everything. Smith, whom Marquina has described as "ultracivilized," has a secret. He is attracted to a woman he has seen in a strange part of the world. He searches her out in a primitive, patriarchal society. Smith attempts to tell people that he has found ways to discover "the secrets of life" but is told that "life only has one secret, and it is in a man's heart" (*Works*,VII,1360). The psychologist falls in love with the woman, whose name is Estrella, and never returns to London. He has decided that life is more meaningful in that primitive society where the heart is still important. This return to a more "natural" life recalls the focus of many of the poems in Marquina's *Odes*.

The same concern for people's ability to love is presented in a different and less simplistic manner in *Adam and Eve in the Dance Hall*, one of Marquina's better stories. Marquina updates the story of Adam and Eve to the post–World War I years. Mr. L. Astoroth — L. for Lucifer — ,who is really the devil, vainly attempts to initiate an affair between Mey, the Countess of Platten and Iob Suárez, who have just met in the Ceibo Dancing Room, although they feel that they knew each other previously. The author's concern is summarized by a secondary character, Mam'zelle, who states that "the intimate and true happiness of love is not of our times" (*Works*,VII,1177). Mey rejects Iob's amorous advances as she tells him that times have changed since Adam and Eve: "What do you expect from a simple, fresh apple after the cocktail?" (*Works*, VII,1185).

In *Women's Souls*, Marquina grouped together in his complete works four narratives which, although written during different periods, have a common theme: the author's interest in the effects of modern times on the female psyche (*Works*,VII,1378–82). Marquina is concerned about the direction taken by women's personalities in "the transitional times" in which they are living, and particularly their new attitudes toward love as old mores are left behind (*Works*,VII,1380–81). The author classifies these four narratives as "studies" because "they lack the simple, dynamic agility of a short story" and "the method and architecture of the novel" (Works, VII,1378).

Marquina traces in Motherhood, published in 1917, the evolution of the Countess of Torre Santana, an egotistical woman "who adored herself through her son, who was the image of his mother" (Works, VII,698). The author explains that although she had given birth, because of her self-centeredness she was still only a "woman." "Motherhood is not only giving birth. It is something else. There are women who are born mothers. There are grandmothers who are still women. Motherhood is not an act, it is a category. It is not flesh: it is a spirit of sacrifice" (Works,VII,733). As Marquina points out, only when the Countess learned to love her son for himself and not for egotistical reasons did she truly begin to become a mother.

The second "study," En la extrema linde (On the Brink), is somewhat less conventional. In On the Brink Marquina states that "women's hearts and minds are changing around us without our noticing it. In abnormal times of change there is a profusion of sketchily outlined individuals that appear to be experiments, Nature's trial attempts toward a new direction. Some triumph, others fall defeated. . . . The latter reach 'the brink' where there is no going farther. . . . Marita Santelmo is one of these characters" (Works, VII,738). The author adds that the first years of Marita's life coincided with that fictitious external and physical movement of independence that has preceded in all countries that so-called liberation of the feminine soul. She took advantage of and abused that independence . . . " (Works,VII,738).[9]

Marita Santelmo in On the Brink sees herself as the redeemer of her "female companions in slavery" and attempts to save her friend Carmen Bove from the donjuanesque Pepe Torno (Works,VII,738). Her efforts end tragically. While riding on Pepe's motorcycle she intentionally causes it to turn over, thinking that both would die. However, only Pepe dies, and Carmen comes to realize, we assume, the error of her ways.

Marquina does not seem to have much sympathy for Marita as a representative of women's liberation. He depicts her as being blinded by her obsessive desire for independence and by her misguided efforts to do things traditionally forbidden to women. The melodramatic incident of the motorcycle is not credible in terms of her expressed desire to prevent Pepe from taking advantage of

Carmen. Viewed from the 1970's, it becomes apparent that Marquina was too "traditional" in his concept of women — as we have observed in his theater — to understand a character like Marita Santelmo.

In *La misa azul (The Blue Mass)*, the third narrative in *Women's Souls*, Marquina studies the personality of Gloria, a vain woman so absorbed in herself that she has little or no love for those surrounding her. Jorge, an unbalanced handyman, believes she is a goddess due to her resemblance to a Greek statue found in the local ruins. This feeds Gloria's vanity, and she does nothing to change his opinion. The demented Jorge, who hears that at one time men had turned on the gods, tries unsuccessfully to kill her and soon thereafter commits suicide, a victim of Gloria's vanity.

In *Un caballero desconocido (An Unknown Gentleman)*, the last of the four "studies" in *Women's Souls*, the protagonist, Margarita is out of touch with the times. While she believes that finding a husband is an affair of the heart, the young ladies around her have a materialistic attitude. Her friends have decided that "oversentimentality of love, the restlessness and demands of the heart, 'happiness' as it is understood in novels and as understood by Margarita, are unrelated to today's life. . . . They have heard that life and women — above all women — have changed radically in the first quarter of the century, and they believe it, like so much society gossip, as if it were the gospel truth" (*Works*, VII, 819). Marquina's point of view can, of course, be anticipated. True happiness can only be found if we continue in the traditional way of letting our hearts be our guide. Margarita finds the ideal man, the "unknown gentleman" she would see during her nights at the concerts.

One of Marquina's better short stories is *Un niño malo (A Bad Boy)*. The work is unique in that the usually omniscient author Marquina delineates his character from within, developing a psychological study of a disturbed child. The story is structured around some papers "found" by the author, written by the fictional Juan de Rincón. The latter describes his childhood starting with his first knowledge of the world acquired through sensations and the feeling of "exclusion" he began to experience as he grew older. He sees his infancy as a "tragedy" compared to no other that life could offer. Later he became a "bad boy": "I'm a disobedient boy, lazy, ungovernable, with a sullen and wicked character. My function is to disobey, even worse, to do the contrary of what I'm told" (*Works*,

VII,1100).   His anguish leads him to try to burn down the house
with himself and the family in it. He does not succeed, but his
parents finally realize that the child is suffering and attempt to make
amends.

These, briefly, are the highlights of Marquina's able characterization of Rincón. Only at times does the author go astray and make
judgments hardly characteristic of a child. Children are almost completely absent from Marquina's literary production, which generally
concentrates on adult female protagonists. The successful results of
this effort to penetrate a child's world would seem to indicate that
Marquina had a talent he did not exploit.

Before completing this survey of Marquina's more notable short
narratives, mention should be made of two additional stories which
have some relevance to his dramatic production.[10] Benvenuto Cellini, the protagonist of Marquina's drama of the same name appears
as a secondary character in the first of these stories, The Other Side
of the Medal. The author has maintained essentially the same concept of the Renaissance artist in both the drama and the story.
Cellini is very sure of himself and of the excellence of his art. He
does not budge in his relations with the Duke Cosme to whom he
hands over four chapters — invented by Marquina and that form
the body of the story — intended for inclusion in his autobiography.
The structure of The Other Side of the Medal is uneven and disjointed, its most interesting aspect (besides the re-appearance of
Cellini) being Marquina's poetic evocation of Renaissance Florence.
The second of these stories is Like the Bees, a conventional narrative
with a rural setting. Written in 1915 and published the following
year, the work anticipates Marquina's return to rural dramas during
the 1920's. The author had initiated his dramatic career with a
number of works in a rural setting around the turn of the century
but had not produced any after 1905. Like the Bees utilizes the
hackneyed theme of the good daughter versus bad step-mother and
is of little general interest beyond its relation to Marquina's theater.

Our survey of Marquina's narratives confirms that the author's
talents were constrained by a genre that did not allow his poetic
muse full rein. Plots, themes, and characters are generally presented within a conventional realistic setting. Over and beyond
considerations of genre, it is evident that Marquina reaches his
highest level of artistic expression in those few narratives imbued
with a poetic quality.

CHAPTER 12

Résumé and Conclusion

M ARQUINA's place in the history of Spanish literature must be decided essentially by the worth of his theater. Although he had in him the makings of an admirable lyric poet and contributed to the Modernist movement's search for new poetic forms in Spain, he chose to divert his energies after 1910 to drama. This choice was influenced by the author's dependence on the income produced by his theater. Marquina's early poems reveal both the young author's sincere lyric voice and his rebellious spirit. Gradually, however, he evolved toward a conservative, traditionalist point of view, and by 1910, when, as he has indicated, he "had found himself," the rebel had disappeared. The author's coming to terms with himself and with the world around him lessened the poetic potential manifest in his early compositions. Although Marquina wrote poems intermittently after 1910, with few exceptions, the lyric voice is missing.

The author's novels and stories were also written mainly during his early career and appeared only infrequently after he had established himself on the Spanish stage. It is evident that prose narratives were unsuited to Marquina's talents: he reaches his highest artistic level in those few narratives that are imbued with a lyrical quality. However, these narratives would be more aptly described as prose poems rather than novels or stories. Generally, plots, themes, and characters are presented within a conventional realistic framework. The rebellious spirit of Marquina's early poems and plays is notably absent in his narratives, as he began to write his prose works when that spirit had begun to ebb.

Today Marquina is usually identified exclusively as the author of historical verse plays that glorify Spain's past. The origin of this erroneous popular notion is found in the predominance of historical plays within his dramatic production and the fact that his early success was achieved with this type of play. His theater, in fact, offers considerable variety and his best works are not found among his historical plays, but among his religious and rural dramas. Moreover, Marquina does not always select glorious historical events; some plays — including his most famous work, *The Sun Has Set in Flanders* which deals with the loss of the Low Countries — are structured around events that are far from illustrious. However, regardless of the historical period, Marquina manages to extol the virtues of the Spanish people.

Over and beyond individual considerations of the theatrical value of Marquina's plays, his popularity as a dramatist was aided by a series of factors. The patriotic focus of his plays written around 1908–1910 found a propitious climate among theater audiences after Spain's disastrous war with the United States. The lyric quality which imbued all literary genres, including the theater, at the turn of the century paved the way for the type of drama Marquina was attempting to establish. In addition, starting in 1908 the author had the backing of María Guerrero and Fernando Díaz de Mendoza who headed the most prestigious theatrical company of the times.

Marquina adjusted his plays to the tastes and ideology of the theater audiences. These audiences found in the author a dramatic style that served to reconfirm their own conservative ideals. The rebel dramatist of the turn of the century had become an exponent of traditionalism. The author created for his theater what amounted to a personal following that applauded his plays during the length of his career. Marquina and many other dramatists of the times, such as Jacinto Benavente, succumbed to commercialization. Those authors who did not follow the accepted theatrical style of the day and attempted to create a more significant dramaturgy (Valle-Inclán, Unamuno, Azorín, and Jacinto Grau), found it almost impossible to stage their plays. García Lorca was a notable exception in that he managed to obtain popular success without compromising his aesthetic principles.

As with the production of many "commercialized" dramatists, Marquina's plays today hold an essentially historical interest. Those plays too rooted in the circumstances of the day have aged rapidly, and other times and other authors have surpassed them.

While Marquina wrote some mediocre plays, he also wrote excellent ones, and to arrive at a just evaluation of his theater both aspects must be considered within the framework of the times during which the plays were created. There are sufficent plays of high caliber within his dramatic production to assure his place in the history of contemporary Spanish theater. Moreover, his initial efforts were directly responsible for the renaissance of Spain's twentieth-century poetic theater, and he was the genre's most assiduous exponent.

Notes and References

Chapter One

1. More complete information on Marquina's life is available in the following biography: José Montero Alonso, *Vida de Eduardo Marquina* (Madrid, 1965). Another valuable source is the author's uncompleted memoirs which cover the period from infancy through 1900: Eduardo Marquina, *Días de infancia y adolescencia: Memorias del último tercio del siglo* (Barcelona, 1964).

2. José Luis Comellas, *Historia de España moderna y contemporánea (1474–1965)* (Madrid, 1967), p. 504.

3. Raymond Carr, *España 1808–1939*, 2nd ed. (Barcelona, 1970), p. 417.

4. Guillermo Díaz-Plaja, *Modernismo frente a Noventa y Ocho*, 2nd ed. (Madrid, 1966), p. 319.

5. Ibid., p. 318.

6. Marquina, p. 112.

7. Jean Bécarud and Gilles Lapouge, *Los anarquistas españoles* (Barcelona, 1972), pp. 45–50.

8. Díaz-Plaja, p. 25.

9. Marquina, pp. 168–169.

10. Ibid., p. 182. According to Marquina in the autobiographical sketch included in Gerardo Diego's anthology *Poesía española contemporánea* (Madrid, 1962), p. 112, he also briefly studied law. However, he does not mention this fact in his memoirs, nor does his biographer José Montero Alonso make any such reference.

11. Marquina's literary vocation might have been influenced by his dramatist uncle Pedro Marquina who achieved minor success around the 1870's.

12. Marquina, p. 183.

13. Ibid.

14. Díaz-Plaja, p. 179.

15. Marquina, p. 184.

16. Ibid., pp. 164–166. The title's play on words is not translatable.

"Guerrita" was the nickname of the bullfighter, Rafael Guerra whose ability the authors defended. His nickname also happens to mean "little war." Neither the pamphlet nor its date of publication is available. Marquina only states that it was written around the time of the Cuban War, which was around 1895. Marquina and de Zulueta also published in 1899 a dramatic poem titled *Jesús y el diablo* (*Jesus and the Devil*).

17. Marquina, p. 186.

18. During other trips to Madrid, Marquina met Unamuno, Pérez de Ayala and Ortega y Gasset.

19. Marquina had learned Catalan outside of his household, as Castilian was the language spoken at home. Although born and raised in Barcelona, he was not an advocate of Catalan separatism, a point of view he defended in a series of three articles published in the Madrid daily *El Imparcial* on June 24th, 25th, and July 1, 1901.

20. Montero Alonso, p. 240.

21. These articles, which covered the author's childhood and adolescence, were collected and published in 1965 in a volume entitled *Días de infancia y adolescencia*. (See Note 1 in this chapter.)

22. The following outline is intended to be a very general guide and does not pretend to be all-encompassing: The so-called "Generation of 98" is a name originally coined by Gabriel Maura and popularized by Azorín in 1913 to describe those turn-of-the-century Spanish writers whose work was influenced by Spain's disastrous war with the United States in 1898. These writers are characterized by their common preoccupation with the "problem of Spain" as they turned a critical eye toward the nation's history and culture, searching for answers that could explain the causes that led to the "Disaster of 1898." Some authors who are generally associated with this concept are Unamuno, Machado, Baroja, Azorín and Maeztu. Although the term "Generation of 1898" has been established in Spanish literary history, its limits are rather hazy and its very existence questionable. Indeed some writers generally linked to "98" such as Baroja and Maeztu have denied its existence. In many cases, there are greater differences among its supposed members than there are similarities.

The boundaries of "Modernism" are somewhat more difficult to define than those of the "Generation of 98." While the latter movement is limited to Spain, the former includes both Spain and Spanish America. Its prime mover was the Nicaraguan poet, Rubén Darío, whose influence found a predisposed audience in Spain among writers searching for new forms of literary expression. Darío, who fused in his work the Hispanic tradition with elements taken from the French Parnassians and Symbolists, brought to Spain marvelous innovations in language and poetry. He opened a world of brilliant new forms, sounds, and rhythms. The Naturalist-Realist mode was replaced by a literature that was generally characterized by its ethereal, exotic nature. Among the writers whose work in one degree or another is associated with Modernism we find Marquina, Juan Ramón Jiménez, Manuel Machado, Valle-Inclán, and Villaespesa.

Both movements existed roughly at the same time and both are found in the works of many writers such as Marquina, Benavente, and Valle-Inclán. Differentiating factors generally mentioned are that Modernism was essentially a poetic, literary movement that included both Spain and Spanish America while the Generation of 1898 was a strictly national current, characterized by its introspective, critical point of view.

23. Marcelino C. Peñuelas has studied this problem of a writer whose works contain elements from both Modernism and Generation of 98 in *Jacinto Benavente* (New York, 1968), pp. 49–61.

24. Hans Jeschke, *La Generación de 1898* (Madrid, 1954), pp. 85–86.

25. Pedro Salinas, "La literatura moderna española," in *Ensayos de literatura hispánica* (Madrid, 1961), pp. 282–83.

26. Pedros Salinas, "Una antología de la poesía española," in *Literatura española siglo XX*, 2nd ed. (México, 1949), p. 143.

27. Pedro Laín Entralgo, *España como problema* (Madrid, 1962), p. 367.

28. Luis Granjel, *Panorama de la generación del 98* (Madrid, 1959), p. 64.

29. Díaz-Plaja, p. 117.

30. Angel Valbuena Prat, *Historia del teatro español* (Barcelona, 1956), p. 606.

31. Angel Valbuena Prat, *Historia de la literatura española* (Barcelona, 1957), III, 400.

32. Ricardo Gullón, *Direcciones del modernismo* (Madrid, 1963), pp. 7–8.

33. Ibid., p. 8.

34. Ibid., p. 20.

Chapter Two

1. The following statement by Federico de Onís is representative of this attitude: "After 1902 he began to write theatrical works, trying out different types of plays, until 1908 when with *The Daughters of the Cid* he found the type of drama that fit his poetic talent." "Eduardo Marquina," in *España en América* (Puerto Rico, 1955), p. 528.

2. Around 1901 Marquina wrote *Emporium* (Barcelona, 1906), a "lyric drama" in Catalan with music by Enrique Morera. The play, which has a historical setting, was never produced.

3. Marquina's literary production has been gathered together and published in the following edition: *Obras Completas (Complete Works)*, 8 vols. (Madrid: Aguilar, 1944–1951). This is the edition cited throughout the present study. Marquina's statement may be found in vol. I, ix.

4. Hereafter subsequent volume and page references to Marquina's *Complete Works* will be included parenthetically in the text and will be indicated by the word *Works*.

5. Anonymous review of *The Shepard* in *Heraldo de Madrid* (February 28, 1902).

6. See Carlos Blanco Aguinaga, *Juventud del 98* (Madrid, 1970); Rafael Pérez de la Dehesa, *Política y sociedad en el primer Unamuno: 1894–1904* (Madrid, 1966).

7. Juan Valera had suggested to Marquina that he create a new type of Don Juan based on Cristobal Lozano's seventeenth-century work, *Soledades de la vida y desengaño del mundo*.

8. *Ne'er-do-well* is not included in Marquina's *Complete Works* but is available in the following edition: *Mala cabeza* (Madrid, 1906).

9. Pilar Díez-Jiménez Castellanos, "Las mujeres en el teatro de Marquina," *Universidad*, XXV (1940), 229.

10. Isabel Snyder, ed., *El monje blanco* by Eduardo Marquina (New Orleans, 1951), p. 4.

11. Manuel Bueno, *Heraldo de Madrid* (March 25, 1906).

Chapter Three

1. "Verse theater" and "poetic theater" are not synonymous although there is an erroneous tendency to use these terms interchangeably. The term "poetic" implies an aesthetic appraisal, whereas "verse" only indicates the medium of expression used. In the case of twentieth-century Spanish drama, "poetic theater" is used, somewhat freely, to designate all those plays written in verse, although there are obviously works included in this designation in which the poetic content is limited. In our study we will continue to use the generally established designation "poetic theater," but the term's limitations should be remembered.

2. This listing, by no means complete, obviously includes authors of widely varying artistic ability. The common denominator is that all wrote plays in verse. Today, besides the major figures of Valle-Inclán, García Lorca and the Machados, only Marquina, Villaespesa and perhaps Fernández Ardavín are remembered.

3. There are, of course, exceptions. Some plays have a rural setting, or at times, an oriental locale such as Francisco Villaespesa's *El alcázar de las perlas (The Palace of the Pearls)* and Marquina's *Erase una vez en Bagdad (Once Upon a Time in Baghdad)*. On occasion, the play takes place in a setting contemporary to the author's time. However, the dramatists generally set their plays far away in space and/or time in order to make their verse more acceptable to the modern audience already used to prose.

4. Angel Valbuena Prat, *Historia del teatro español* (Barcelona, 1956), p. 606.

5. José García Mercadal, ed., *Troteras y Danzaderas*, (Madrid, 1966), p. 14; Andrés Amorós, *Vida y literatura en "Troteras y Danzaderas"* (Madrid, 1973), pp. 193–205.

6. Unpublished letters by Ramón Pérez de Ayala to Eduardo Marquina in the possesion of the dramatist's son, Luis Marquina, in Madrid.

7. Gonzalo Torrente Ballester, *Panorama de la literatura española contemporánea*, 2nd ed. (Madrid, 1961), I, 137–38.

8. Guillermo Díaz-Plaja, *Modernismo frente a Noventa y Ocho*, 2nd ed. (Madrid, 1966), p. 125. Marquina's poetry of this period also reflects this patriotic spirit, particularly in the collection *Canciones del momento (Songs of the Moment)*, published in 1910. (*Works* VI, 297–427)

9. Valbuena Prat, p. 601.

10. John Gasner, *Masters of the Drama* (New York, 1957), p. 412.

11. Eduardo Marquina, "Mi primera emoción," *ABC* (Madrid, March 2, 1912).

12. Ramón Menéndez Pidal, *La epopeya catellana a través de la literatura española* (Buenos Aires, 1945), p. 238.

13. The play was also dedicated to the famous actors, María Guerreno and her husband Fernando Díaz de Mendoza, who premiered the play.

14. Manuel Bueno, *Heraldo de Madrid* (Madrid, March 6, 1908).

15. Menéndez Pidal, pp. 238–39.

16. Menéndez Pidal, p. 238.

17. The play (like *The Daughters of the Cid*) is also dedicated to María Guerrero and Fernando Díaz de Mendoza who had selected *Doña María the Intrepid* as the inaugural drama for the newly renovated Princesa Theater, which had recently become the property of the famous actors.

18. Ruth Lansing and Milagros de Alda, eds., *La morisca* by Eduardo Marquina (Philadelphia, 1927), p. viii.

19. Sturgis E. Leavitt, ed., *Las flores de Aragón* by Eduardo Marquina (New York and London, 1928), p. ix.

20. El Caballero Audaz, "Eduardo Marquina," *Galería*, 3rd ed. (Madrid: 1946), I, 593.

21. Quoted by José Montero Alonso, *Vida de Eduardo Marquina* (Madrid, 1965), p. 152.

22. The year 1910 must be kept in mind as the exact date. Marquina's complete works erroneously list 1909. (*Works*, I, 800)

23. Montero Alonso, pp. 153–56.

24. Ernest H. Hespelt and Primitivo R. Sanjurjo, eds., *En Flandes se ha puesto el sol.* Introduction by Federico de Onís (D. C. Heath, 1924), p. 199.

25. Federico de Onís in Hespelt and Sanjurjo, p. xv.

26. Gonzalo Torrente Ballester *Teatro español contemporáneo*, 2nd. ed. (Madrid, 1968), p. 380.

27. Federico de Onís, p. xv.

28. Fernando Lazaro Carreter, "Apuntes sobre el teatro de García Lorca," *Papeles de Son Armadans*, 52 (July 1960), 19.

29. Ibid., 18.

30. "Eduardo Marquina," *La estafeta literaria*, 15 (February 1945), 15.

Chapter Four

1. Having Philip IV dismiss the Conde Duque immediately after the loss of Portugal is an anachronism. The Conde Duque was not dismissed until approximately two years later, around January 1643.

2. Azorín. Quoted by Guillermo Díaz-Plaja, *Modernismo frente a Noventa y Ocho*, 2nd ed. (Madrid, 1966), p. 94.

3. Manuel Bueno, *Heraldo de Madrid* (December 1, 1914).

4. Manuel Bueno, *Heraldo de Madrid* (March 31, 1916).

5. Quoted by Constancio Eguía Ruiz, "Tradición y evolución en el teatro de Eduardo Marquina," *Razón y Fe*, 97 (1931), 345.

6. Ibid.

Chapter Five

1. In spite of Marquina's statement as to his "systematic" use of verse, he did write two more prose plays: *La reina del mundo (The Queen of the World)* and *Lo que Dios no perdona (What God Does Not Forgive)*, premièred in 1928 and 1935 respectively.

2. Marquina's religious dramas *El monje blanco (The White Monk)*, *Teresa de Jesús* and *María la viuda (María the Widow)* premièred in 1930, 1932, and 1943 respectively, have historical settings, but their aesthetic and ideological background is quite different. They cannot be classified with such plays as *The Sun Has Set in Flanders* and *The Great Captain*.

3. This change in setting was influenced by the dramatist Gregorio Martínez Sierra who, according to Marquina, had taken part in the creation of both *The Peacock* and *A Night in Venice* and "never wished to appear as collaborator." (*Works*, IV, 1351)

4. Enrique de Mesa, *Apostillas a la escena* (Madrid, 1929), p. 281.

5. In 1925, in collaboration with the Cuban author Alfonso Henández Catá, Marquina wrote *Don Luis Mejía*, based on the character of the same name in José Zorrilla's *Don Juan Tenorio*. While the play does have a historical setting, it has a direct literary basis and does not fall precisely in the category of dramas in the line of *The Sun Has Set in Flanders*. (See also Note 2 in this chapter.)

6. Quoted by Enrique Díez-Canedo in his review of the play's première: *La Voz* (Madrid, October 30, 1935).

7. Alfredo Marquerie, *ABC* (Madrid, January 4, 1946); Raimundo de los Reyes, "Movimiento literario: Teatro," *Cuadernos de Literatura* (Enero-Febrero 1947), p. 130.

8. Before completing this survey of Marquina's historical theater, mention should be made of *Susona de Santa Cruz*, an unfinished play begun in conjunction with the historian José Andrés Vásquez in the 1920's. The play, set in Seville, deals with the love between Susona, daughter of the Jewish leader Diego Susón, and the Christian, don Adalíd de Guzmán. The incomplete manuscript was published posthumously in *Archivo Hispalense*, 22, no. 39–41 (1950), 93–129.

Chapter Six

1. The three main categories of Marquina's theater are: historical, rural, and religious dramas.

2. Angel Valbuena Prat, "Modernismo y Generación del 98 en la literatura española," in *Historia general de las literaturas hispánicas*, ed. Guillermo Díaz-Plaja (Barcelona, 1967), VI, 214.

3. Francisco García Pavón has studied this subject and its repercussions in Spanish theater in *Teatro social en España* (Madrid, 1962).

4. Enrique Díez-Canedo, *El Sol* (Madrid, March 30, 1924).

5. Eduardo Marquina in an interview published on the date of *The Poor Little Carpenter*'s première, in *El Imparcial* (Madrid, March 29, 1924).

6. This quality was apparently evident in its first performance as Enrique Díez-Canedo encountered a similar difficulty in describing the play: "To relate in prose the 'folk tale' that Marquina told from the stage of the Princess Theater perhaps is not possible." *El Sol* (Madrid, March 30, 1924).

7. Ibid.

8. Eduardo Marquina, *Días de infancia y adolescencia: Memorias del último tercio del siglo XIX* (Barcelona, 1964), p. 50.

9. Enrique Díez-Canedo, *El Sol* (Madrid, February 11, 1927).

10. Valbuena Prat, 214.

11. Enrique de Mesa, *Apostillas a la escena* (Madrid, 1929), p. 307–8.

12. Ibid., p. 308.

13. In *Salvadora*, as in his early rural dramas, Marquina again makes use of a folk song to illustrate the dramatic action. This device was used successfully by Lope de Vega and, among others, by Jacinto Benavente and Federico García Lorca.

14. Carlos Fernández Cuesta, *La Epoca* (Madrid, January 18, 1931).

Chapter Seven

1. Angel Valbuena Prat, *Historia del teatro español* (Barcelona, 1956), p. 610.

2. José Montero Alonso ed., *Teresa de Jesús* by Eduardo Marquina (Salamanca, 1964), p. 19.

3. See (*Works*, IV, 1349–50), where Marquina makes special note of the importance of the plastic arts in the play's composition.

4. Angel Valbuena Prat, "Modernismo y Generación del 98 en la literatura española," in *Historia general de las literaturas hispánicas*, ed. Guillermo Díaz-Plaja (Barcelona, 1967), VI, 215; 236.

5. Ibid., 216.

6. Ibid., 217.

7. Montero Alonso, *Teresa de Jesús*, p. 15.

8. Eduardo Marquina, "Teresa de Jesús," *Heraldo de Madrid*, November 25, 1932. See Montero Alonso, *Teresa de Jesús*, pp. 20–21, for a detailed synopsis of the play's historical background. Also of interest are Marquina's notes on both the trilogy and *Teresa de Jesús* (*Works*, I, 1239–43) and (*Works*, IV, 1352).

9. Quoted by Montero Alonso, *Teresa de Jesús*, p. 17.

10. Eduardo Marquina, "Teresa de Jesús," *Heraldo de Madrid*, November 25, 1932.

11. Isabel Snyder ed., *El monje blanco* by Eduardo Marquina (New Orleans, 1951), p. 7.

12. "La figura de Santa Teresa en el teatro español," *La estafeta literaria*, 453–54 (October 1970), 55.

13. The plays Marquina wrote during this period are *In the Name of the Father, San Martín's Flag, The Holy Brotherhood*, and *El estudiante endiablado (The Devilish Student)*, all staged between 1935 and 1942.

14. José Montero Alonso, *Vida de Eduardo Marquina* (Madrid, 1965), p. 262.

15. Ibid, p. 246. See also Ramón Menéndez Pidal, *Estudios literarios*, 8th ed. (Madrid, 1957), pp. 78–79.

16. Quoted by Montero Alonso, *Vida*, p. 261.

17. Nicolás González Ruiz, *La cultura española en los últimos veinte años: El teatro* (Madrid, 1949), pp. 17–18.

18. Pilar Díez-Jiménez Castellanos, "Las mujeres en el teatro de Marquina," *Universidad*, 25 (1948), 227.

19. Valbuena Prat, *Historia del teatro español*, p. 616.

Chapter Eight

1. Marquina's contemporary plays had a precursor entitled *Mala cabeza (Ne'er-do-well)* among his early dramas.

2. Although *The Princess Amuses Herself* is written in prose, it does not fall within the category of Marquina's contemporary plays. The work is analyzed along with the author's miscellaneous plays.

3. Unpublished letter from don Luis Marquina to the author of this study.

4. Ibid.

5. *Vixen* was premièred in 1919 according to the information provided by Marquina's son, don Luis Marquina, in the same letter cited in notes 3 and 4.

6. Enrique de Mesa, *Apostillas a la escena* (Madrid, 1929), p. 310.

7. Halfdan Gregersen, *Ibsen and Spain: A Study of Comparative Drama* (Cambridge, 1936), pp. 169–70.

Chapter Nine

1. Marquina also translated into Spanish the following plays, all of which are included in his complete works: Dario Nicodemi, *La enemiga (The Enemy)* from Italian; Hugo von Hoffmansthal, *Elektra* from German in collaboration with Joaquín Pena; José María de Segarra, *Fidelidad (Fidelity)* from Catalan; and Freidrich Schiller, *La Conjuración de Fiesco (Fiesco)* from German. Marquina adapted Lope de Vega's *La Dorotea (Dorothea)* for the stage and wrote a new version of *La niña de Gómez Arias (Gómez Arias' Girl)* by Calderón de la Barca. Both plays are also included in Marquina's complete works.

2. Quoted by José Montero Alonso, *Vida de Eduardo Marquina* (Madrid, 1965), p. 285.

3. Pilar Díez-Jiménez Castellanos, "Las mujeres en el teatro de Marquina," *Universidad*, 25 (1948), 219.

4. In France, Edmond Rostand in 1895 wrote *La Princesse lointaine (The Far-Away Princess)* which deals with the love of the troubadour Rudel for the Countess of Tripoli.

5. According to the dramatist's son, don Luis Marquina, in an unpublished letter to the author of this study, the play was premièred during the years 1911–1914.

6. Marquina also used a "play within a play" structure in the first act of his contemporary play, *Without a Weapon*.

7. Pilar Díez-Jiménez Castellanos, p. 221.

8. Enrique Díez-Canedo, *El Sol* (Madrid, February 11, 1932).

9. Enrique Díez-Canedo, *El Sol* (Madrid, January 19, 1928).

10. Although Marquina claims this was his last collaboration, (*Works*, III,1359), he forgets an uncompleted historical play, *Susona de Santa Cruz*, that was started around 1926 with José Andrés Vásquez.

11. Enrique Díez-Canedo, *El Sol* (Madrid, January 18, 1925).

12. "En torno al último Don Juan," *Hispania* (December 1925), p. 356.

13. José de Laserna, *El Imparcial* (Madrid, January 18, 1925); Enrique Díez-Canedo, *El Sol* (Madrid, January 18, 1925).

14. The Don Juan theme has attracted a good many Spanish dramatists during the twentieth century. Some examples are: Miguel de Unamuno, *El hermano Juan (Brother Juan);* Jacinto Grau, *Don Juan de Carillana* and *El burlador que no se burla (The Seducer Who Doesn't Seduce);* Manuel and Antonio Machado, *Juan de Mañara.* Besides *Don Luis Mejía* and *The Devilish Student,* other plays by Marquina that include protagonists with donjuanesque traits are: *Teodora the Nun, One Woman, A Night in Venice, There's More to Life,* and *The Julianes.*

15. Nicolás González Ruiz, *La cultura española en los últimos veinte años: El teatro* (Madrid, 1949), p. 18.

Chapter Ten

1. Marquina had previously published two works in collaboration with Luis de Zulueta: a pamphlet *Lo que España necesita: menos guerra y más Guerrita (What Spain needs: Less War and More Guerrita,* and the dramatic poem, *Jesús y el diablo (Jesus and the Devil).*

2. José Montero Alonso ed., *Teresa de Jesús* by Eduardo Marquina (Salamanca, 1964), p. 11.

3. In reference to Marquina's relation to Modernism and the Generation of 98 see Chapter 1.

4. See Eduardo Juliá Martínez, "Eduardo Marquina, poeta lírico y dramático," *Cuadernos de literatura contemporánea,* nos. 3–4 (1942), 114.

5. The sea, specifically the Mediterranean Sea along the shores of Marquina's native Catalonia, inspired a great many of his poems. The author usually spent his summers in the Catalan village of Cadaqués on the Mediterranean coast in Spain's northeast corner. In answer to the question "What Catalan antecedents do you have in your work?" Marquina has answered as follows: "Personal or pertaining to a school, none. . . . But my works as a whole, above all my poems, and also my theater, are full of sentiments . . . and echoes with a Catalan background. Thus a certain poetry of the home, and of the landscape. . . . Thus the subject of the sea so frequent in my verses; waters, rivers, and mountain springs, and fountains in my poems." See *La estafeta literaria* (February 15, 1945), p. 15.

6. It must be noted, however, that in *Mi huerto en la ladera (My Garden on the Hillside),* a collection of varied poems written over a number of years and published jointly in 1936, the theme of nature figures prominently.

7. Quoted by José Montero Alonso, *Vida de Eduardo Marquina* (Madrid, 1965), pp. 81–82.

8. Quoted by Juliá Martínez, pp. 117–18. Although Marquina cites a number of titles of these projected "Georgic" poems, he never completed the series announced in the epilogue.

9. "Ballad of the Vagabonds" recalls another poem in *Odes* titled "Versos acanallados" ("Vile Verses"). In both compositions Marquina exhorts those "outsiders" such as the vagabonds and beggars, whom he considers victims of society, to rise up and "triumph."

10. Federico de Onís, "Eduardo Marquina," in *España en América* (Puerto Rico, 1955), p. 526.

11. Quoted by Montero Alonso, *Vida de Eduardo Marquina*, p. 114.

12. *Ibid.*, p. 105.

13. The poem is divided into six parts: "Prologue," "Vendimión ermitaño" ("Vendimión the Hermit"), "Vendimión doméstico" ("Domestic Vendimión"), "Verdimión hispánico" ("Hispanic Vendimión"), "Vendimión combatido" ("Embattled Vendimión"), and "Vendimión astral" ("Astral Vendimión"). Given the length of the poem and its many facets we will limit our analysis to the work's most significant aspects.

14. Montero Alonso, *Vida de Eduardo Marquina*, p. 126.

15. Eduardo Gómez de Baquero, "Vendimión, poema por Eduardo Marquina," *La España Moderna*, Año 21, no. 246 (June 1909), 167. The quote "Oh time Vendimión of all the grape harvests!" is found in *Works*, VI,437.

16. Gómez de Baquero, 168.

17. The swan so closely identified with Modernism and Rubén Darío is not one of Marquina's usual symbols.

18. Gómez de Baquero, 171.

19. Gómez de Baquero, 172.

20. Federico de Onís, "Historia de la poesía modernista, 1882–1932," in *España en América* (Puerto Rico, 1955), p. 216.

21. Marquina's son, Luis, was born on May 25, 1904.

Chapter Eleven

1. See Federico Sainz de Robles, "La novela realista y el teatro de costumbres en el siglo XX," in *Historia general de las literaturas hispánicas*, ed. Guillermo Díaz-Plaja (Barcelona, 1967), VI, 451.

2. *Ibid.*

3. Marquina's narratives are contained in Volume VII of his complete works. This volume includes four novels which are grouped together and are the first to appear, and nineteen short narratives, some of which because of their structure and length could be classified as short novels. Marquina, however, simply entitles his volume *Novelas y cuentos (Novels and Stories)* and gives practically no additional information other than to

classify the four short narratives included under the title *Almas de mujer (Women's Souls)* as "studies" since he feels they cannot be described either as novels or stories (i.e., *cuentos*). Since a clear distinction would likely be impossible, for the purpose of this study we shall use short story or story, to refer to those short narratives included in Volume VII.

4. The most lyrical of Marquina's narratives is his novel *Almas anónimas (Anonymous Souls)*. A number of stories have in parts a lyrical "tinge" such as the poetic evocation of Florence and Venice in *El reverso de la medalla (The Other Side of the Medal)* and *La paz en Venecia (The Tranquillity of Venice)*. At times some of his characters are surrounded by a melancholic poetic aura, for example Irene Pombal, the protagonist of *El beso en la herida (Balm on the Wound)*.

5. Marquina explains these divisions in *The Other Side of the Medal* when the author tells us that the Cellini writings have been "divided into small chapters to guide the reader . . ." (*Works*, VII, 1116).

6. A possible exception would be Bernardo Aguilar, a rather decadent Don Juan type—but a good father—who recalls in some aspects Valle-Inclán's Marqués de Bradomín. Another would be the exceptionally well-delineated protagonist in the story, *Un niño malo (A Bad Boy)*.

7. In the notes pertaining to *The Queen is a Woman Too* in Marquina's complete works, the author is obviously aware of past criticisms of his interpretations of historical figures as he attempts to justify his conception of Isabella: "The pages of this novel are written with absolute respect for history although, naturally, outside of it: in the licit and open field of poetic fiction" (*Works*, VII, 1377).

8. It is interesting to observe Marquina's rather discreet interpretation of Gonzalo de Córdoba in the novel. On the few occasions that he appears, the author pictures him as a capable soldier who serves the kings dutifully and respects Isabella as well as Ferdinand. There is no trace of the protagonist of *The Great Captain*, who was in love with Isabella and competed in his own way with Ferdinand. Both *The Great Captain* and the author's very personal conception of the protagonist Gonzalo de Córdoba were severely criticized, all of which prompted Marquina temporarily to abandon historical verse theater in 1916.

9. The date of publication of *On the Brink* is not available. Marquina does not indicate any date in his complete works. However, when he grouped his "studies" under the general title of *Women's Souls* he placed *On the Brink* between *Motherhood* and *La misa Azul (The Blue Mass)*, which were published in 1917 and 1918 respectively. The last "study," *Un caballero desconocido (An Unknown Gentleman)* was not published until 1940.

10. Mention should also be made of Marquina's role as a translator. In addition to those plays listed in the chapter on his miscellaneous theater, Marquina translated into Spanish works by Baudelaire, Verlaine, Victor

Hugo, Chateaubriand, and by the Portuguese authors, Eca de Queiroz and
Guerra Junqueiro. Marquina would also occasionally write essays. A small
number of these have been collected and included in Vol. VIII of his
Complete Works.

Selected Bibliography

Plays

The date following each play is that of its première. Unless otherwise noted, the première took place in Madrid.

1. *The Shepherd (El pastor);* three acts; February 27, 1902.
2. *Still Water (Agua mansa);* zarzuela in four scenes; December 23, 1902. Music by Juan Gay.
3. *The Return of the Flock (La vuelta del rebaño);* zarzuela in four scenes with a prologue; October 30, 1903. Music by Juan Gay.
4. *Ne'er-do-well (Mala cabeza);* three scenes; February 26, 1906.
5. *Benvenuto Cellini;* four acts; March 24, 1906.
6. *The Dauphin (El delfín);* zarzuela in one act and four scenes; February 9, 1907. Written in collaboration with José Salmerón y García. Music by Tomás Barrera and Juan Gay.
7. *The Daughters of the Cid (Las hijas del Cid);* five acts; March 5, 1908.
8. *Doña María the Intrepid (Doña María la brava);* four acts; November 27, 1909.
9. *The Sun Has Set in Flanders (En Flandes se ha puesto el sol);* four acts; Montevideo, July 27, 1910; Madrid, December 18, 1910.
10. *The Last Day (El último día);* one act; April 4, 1911.
11. *The Prioress of Pastrana (La alcaidesa de Pastrana);* one act; May 15, 1911.
12. *The Unbreakable Doll (La muñeca irrompible);* six scenes; Premièred between 1911 and 1914.
13. *The Nun's Letters (Las cartas de la monja);* one act; 1912.
14. *The Troubadour King (El rey trovador);* four acts; February 13, 1912.
15. *The Mask (El antifaz);* one act; May 1, 1912.
16. *Death at Alba (La muerte en Alba);* one act; 1913.
17. *When the Roses Bloom (Cuando florezcan los rosales);* three acts; February 14, 1913.

153

18. *For the King's Sins (Por los pecados del rey)*; three acts; March 22, 1913.
19. *The Armed Hawk (El gavilán de la espada)*; one act; May 1913.
20. *The Altarpiece of Agrellano (El retablo de Agrellano)*; three acts; Oviedo, October 15, 1913; Madrid, November 14, 1913.
21. *Ivy (La hiedra)*; three acts; February 27, 1914.
22. *The Flowers of Aragón (Las flores de Aragón)*; four acts; November 30, 1914.
23. *One Woman (Una mujer)*; three acts; January 11, 1915.
24. *The Great Captain (El Gran Capitán)*; three acts; March 30, 1916.
25. *Skylark (Alondra)*; three acts; April 5, 1918. Unpublished.
26. *Mr. Night Flower (Dondiego de noche)*; two acts; 1919.
27. *Vixen (Alimaña)*; four acts; 1919.
28. *The Princess Amuses Herself (La princesa juega)*; two acts; 1920.
29. *Ebora*; three acts; 1921.
30. *The Peacock (El pavo real)*; three acts; November 14, 1922.
31. *A French Rose (Rosa de Francia)*; three acts; March 31, 1923. Written in collaboration with Luis Fernández Ardavín.
32. *A Night in Venice (Una noche en Venecia)*; four acts with a prologue; November 19, 1923.
33. *The Road to Happiness (El camino de la felicidad)*; three acts with a prologue; Barcelona, 1924; Madrid, January 18, 1928. Written in collaboration with Gregorio Martínez Sierra.
34. *The Poor Little Carpenter (El pobrecito carpintero)*; four acts; March 29, 1924.
35. *Don Luis Mejía*; three acts and an epilogue; January 17, 1925. Written in collaboration with Alfonso Hernández Catá.
36. *Blessed Fruit (Fruto bendito)*; three acts; January 8, 1927.
37. *The Hermitage, the Fountain, and the River (La ermita, la fuente y el río)*; three acts; February 10, 1927.
38. *There's More to Life (La vida es más)*; three acts; April 7, 1928.
39. *Without a Weapon (Sin horca ni cuchillo)*; three acts; April 5, 1929.
40. *Salvadora*; three acts; October 11, 1929.
41. *The White Monk (El monje blanco)*; three acts; February 5, 1930.
42. *Hidden Spring (Fuente escondida)*; three acts; January 17, 1931.
43. *Once Upon a Time in Baghdad (Era una vez en Bagdad)*; three acts; February 10, 1932.
44. *The Julianes (Los Julianes)*; three acts; May 13, 1932.
45. *Teresa de Jesús*; six "Impressions"; November 25, 1932.
46. *What God Does Not Forgive (Lo que Dios no perdona)*; three acts; March 22, 1935. Unpublished.
47. *In the Name of the Father (En el nombre del padre)*; three acts; October 28, 1935.

48. *San Martín's Flag (La bandera de San Martín);* one act; Buenos Aires, May 25, 1937.
49. *The Holy Brotherhood (La Santa Hermandad);* two acts with a prologue; Santiago, Chile, May 1937.
50. *The Devilish Student (El estudiante endiablado);* three acts; February 12, 1942.
51. *María the Widow (María la viuda);* two acts; October 22, 1943.
52. *The Galleon and the Miracle (El galeón y el milagro);* five "chapters"; January 3, 1946.

Plays Not Performed
The date following each play is the year of composition.
1. *Emporium;* lyric drama in three acts; written around 1901 and published in 1906; in Catalán with music by Enric Morera.
2. *A Place in the Mountains (Rincón de montaña);* three acts; 1905.
3. *Teodora the Nun (La monja Teodora);* three "parts"; 1905.
4. *A Certain Face (El rostro del ideal);* four acts; 1910.
5. *Story of a Wedding and the Challenge of the Devil (Cuento de una boda y desafío del diablo);* three acts with a prologue and epilogue; 1910.
6. *Mountain Song (Cantiga de Serrana);* one act; 1914.
7. *The Morisca (La morisca);* lyric drama in one act; 1914.
8. *The Stranger (La extraña);* three acts; 1919.
9. *The Queen of the World (La reina del mundo);* three acts; 1928.

Unpublished Plays Attributed to Marquina
Only incomplete information is available on the following plays.
1. *Greece's Laughter (La risa de Grecia);* premièred in 1905.
2. *The Phantom Fan (El abanico duende)* "musical comedy" written in 1918 with the collaboration of Amadeo Vives.
3. *Aphrodite's Necklace (El collar de Afrodita);* "Operetta bufa in three acts"; premièred in Madrid, April 17, 1925. Music by Jacinto Guerrero y Torres.
4. *The Image (La Imagen);* three acts; premièred in Madrid, May 10, 1929. In collaboration with Diego Amiel Durand and Joaquín Guichot.

Complete Works
Marquina's literary production has been collected and published as *Obras completas (Complete Works)* in eight volumes by Aguilar (Madrid, 1944–1951). Vols. I–VII were published in 1944, and Marquina actively supervised their preparation. Vol. VIII was published posthumously in 1951. The breakdown of the eight volumes is as follows: Vols. I–V, theater; Vol. VI, poetry; Vol. VII, novels and short stories; Vol. VIII, miscellaneous plays, poems, and prose.

For additional information on separate editions of Marquina's individual works, see the extensive bibliography included in the following article: Eduardo Juliá Martínez, "Eduardo Marquina, poeta lírico y dramático," *Cuadernos de literatura española,* nos. 3–4 (1942), 142–50.

Special Editions of Marquina's Plays
All the following editions include an introduction, bibliography, and notes.
The Sun Has Set in Flanders (En Flandes se ha puesto el sol). Ed. Ernest H. Hespelt and Primitivo R. Sanjurjo. Introduction by Federico de Onís. Boston: D. C. Heath, 1924. Textbook edition.
The Morisca (La Morisca). Ed. Ruth Lansing and Milagros de Alda. Philadelphia: The John C. Winston Co., 1927. Textbook edition.
The Flowers of Aragón (Las flores de Aragón). Ed. Sturgis E. Leavitt. New York and London: The Century Company, 1928. Textbook edition.
The White Monk (El monje blanco). Ed. Isabel Snyder. New Orleans, Loyola University of the South, 1951. Textbook edition.
Teresa de Jesús. Ed. José Montero Alonso. Salamanca: Anaya, 1964. Its brief introduction to all of Marquina's works is of particular interest.

SECONDARY SOURCES

The bibliography on Marquina's literary production is quite limited. Most of the existing critical studies deal with the author's theater, while only a very few are devoted to his poetry. Critics have generally passed over Marquina's novels and stories.
BERENGUER CARISOMO, ARTURO. "Algunas impresiones sobre el teatro de Marquina." *Nosotros* (1937), pp. 176–96. Series of wide-ranging comments on highlights of Marquina's theater.
DE LA NUEZ, MANUEL. "El teatro de Eduardo Marquina." Doctoral dissertation. New York University, 1971. Detailed study of Marquina's plays.
DIEZ-CANEDO, ENRIQUE. *Artículos de crítica teatral: El teatro español de 1914 a 1936.* 5 vols. México: Joaquín Mortiz, 1968. II, 9–68. A series of excellent reviews of Marquina's plays by one of Spain's major drama critics.
DIEZ-JIMENEZ CASTELLANOS, PILAR. "Las mujeres en el teatro de Marquina." *Universidad,* XXV (1948), 209–41. Fine study of women in Marquina's theater.
EGUIA-RUIZ, CONSTANCIO. "Tradición y evolución en el teatro de Marquina." *Razón y Fe,* XCVI (1931), 281–290; XCVII (1931), 336–347; XCVIII (1932), 349–360; XCIX (1932), 78–79. A series of overly subjective articles but includes some interesting aspects on development of Marquina's theater.

GARCIA DIAZ, PABLO. "Introducción a la vida y al teatro de Eduardo Marquina." Doctoral dissertation, University of Madrid, 1952. Excellent source of information on Marquina's life and theater.

GOMEZ DE BAQUERO, EDUARDO. "*Vendimión*, poema por Eduardo Marquina." *La España Moderna*, XXI (1909), 163–73. Perceptive article on Marquina's most ambitious and philosophical poetic work.

GONZALEZ-BLANCO, ANDRES. *Los dramaturgos españoles: Primera serie.* Valencia: Editorial Cervantes, 1917. Pp. 295–330. Lacks historical perspective but offers interesting comments on Marquina's first successes as a dramatist.

JULIA MARTINEZ, EDUARDO. "Eduardo Marquina, poeta lírico y dramático." *Cuadernos de literatura contemporánea*, nos. 3–4 (1942), 109–50. Gives a composite view of Marquina as a lyrical and dramatic poet. Contains excellent bibliography.

MESA, ENRIQUE DE. *Apostillas a la escena.* Madrid: Renacimiento, 1929. Pp. 252–58; 280–312. Penetrating studies on Marquina's plays written during the 1920's.

MONTERO ALONSO, JOSE. *Vida de Eduardo Marquina.* Madrid: Editora Nacional, 1965. The only biography on Marquina. Contains many references to his literary production. Indispensable for study of Marquina.

ONIS, FEDERICO DE. "Historia de la poesía modernista, 1882–1932," in *España en América.* Puerto Rico: Universidad de Puerto Rico, 1955. Pp. 215–16. Brief but penetrating comments on Marquina's poems in relation to Modernism and the Generation of 98.

————. "Eduardo Marquina," in *España en América.* Puerto Rico: Universidad de Puerto Rico, 1955. Pp. 525–30. Overall view of Marquina's poetry and theater with perceptive comments on the latter. This article is the same introduction included in the Hespelt and Sanjurjo edition of *The Sun Has Set in Flanders* listed among the primary sources.

ROGERIO SANCHEZ, JOSE. *El teatro poético: Valle-Inclán, Marquina.* Madrid: Sucessores de Hernando, 1914. Lacks historical perspective but includes interesting information of beginnings of poetic theater.

RUIZ RAMON, FRANCISCO. *Historia del teatro español 2, siglo XX.* Madrid: Alianza Editorial, 1971. Pp. 64–71. Excellent compact appraisal of Marquina's plays and their relation to the poetic theater.

VALBUENA PRAT, ANGEL. "Modernismo y Generación del 98 en la literatura española," in *Historia general de las literaturas hispánicas.* Ed. Guillermo Díaz-Plaja. Barcelona: Editorial Vergara, 1967. VI, 210–18. An updating of all his previous studies on Marquina's poetry and theater. Valuable comments on Marquina's religious and rural dramas.

Index